HOPE LINES:

18 Stories of Families in Trouble and the Help They Need in Spirit, Sense, and Law

By Neil Presley Cox

First paperback edition January 2022

Original content by Neil Presley Cox, Attorney
Interior formatting and design by Sandy Dell
Cover by janekorunoski, Fiverr
Cover content and manuscript editing, Mal Dell

Elbow Grease Press

ISBN 978-0-9753676-0-5 (paperback)
Also available as Kindle e-book on Amazon Kindle Store
Also available as digital PDF (including individual stories) at the link below:

https://www.neilpresleycox.com/hopelines.html

For comments and questions please email to:
hopelinesbook@gmail.com

DEDICATION

To my beautiful wife, Anna. Completing this project took many exhausting and challenging moments, as anyone who writes an original work can attest. Your belief in me and your positivity kept me moving forward and on task. I appreciate you so much!

ACKNOWLEDGMENTS

Much thanks and gratitude to Patti Lee, who taught and inspired me throughout the ups and downs of writing ***Hope Lines***. Patti's knowledge and craft were enormously helpful. Even more importantly, Patti cares about people, and her influence on the tone and spirit of ***Hope Lines*** was immeasurable.

Thank you to my brother, Eric. You were a stalwart in sharing ideas and debating philosophies. All your kindnesses to our family helped me soldier on!

Appreciation also, for Mal and Sandy Dell of Elbow Grease Press, new friends who took on the challenges of final editing, printing, and publishing of my greatest work. Now publicly available, I am proud, with their help, to offer ***Hope Lines*** in Kindle e-book, paperback, and PDF editions.

FOREWORD

"The Ultimate Resource Guide for 'Families in Trouble'!"

Neil Presley Cox was writing ***Hope Lines*** when I met him at a local writers' group in Lewiston, Idaho, 2019. We began networking, mostly via social media, where we shared and appreciated our different (but mutual) passion for helping solve every-day realities, with a dose of the spiritual sprinkled into the mix.

Neil possesses rare positive qualities for any attorney, and more so for one who works almost daily with families in trouble, even crisis, without becoming jaded. (Well, mostly—be sure to catch his story of personal "demons" in the Preface section.)

As a Licensed Spiritual Practitioner serving clients in search of life-coaching, I immediately connected to the depth of knowledge, sincerity, and down-to-earth approach in ***Hope Lines***. Neil intuitively offers HOPE while throwing LINES of rescue to your current (or future) situation, inside this landmark resource.

Over time, I became fascinated with the book's entire concept: mixing fictional, but common, short stories of woe, with practical solutions addressing these challenges. His 18 engaging dramas provide templates covering the most common legal, behavioral, and relational issues in today's personal and family environments.

As our friendship grew, both I (and my husband) fell in love with Neil and his work, so we even offered—and Neil accepted—to launch his book under our small publishing imprint.

Each of the 18 tragic sagas includes a relevant biblical citation, and ends with sections on reflection, application, and a "resource toolbox". Other content includes five "Calls for New Hope and Faith", plus a couple bonus samples of "addiction recovery poetry", from the future 2nd edition of his first book, ***Alcoholprism***.

In a world increasingly filled with confusion and strife, Neil's quarter-century as a family attorney, his own successful recovery from alcohol addiction, and a lifetime of Christian/spiritual perspective, makes Neil uniquely qualified to write this book.

For you and loved ones facing legal, emotional, or behavioral challenges, it becomes a great relief to find answers in this informative, entertaining (and sometimes painfully close-to-home) manual of life. And, if like most, you relate to some of these stories from a current or past perspective, it may even make you cry, as it did for me.

As an unexpected bonus to my own work, the opportunities to apply Neil's stories and resources during client sessions are more plentiful than I imagined. And to great advantage, considering client responses. Any flavor of counselor, minister, or psychiatrist could add this book to their professional library with equal benefit.

Please remember that regardless of the situation, **YOU ARE NOT ALONE**. ***Hope Lines*** will help you discover pathways to answers and resulting lower stress levels when troubles rear their ugly head. Representing the Ultimate Resource Guide for families in trouble or crisis, I believe strongly that ***Hope Lines*** should be on the bookshelf or coffee table of every home with current relational issues (or in anticipation of nipping future challenges in the bud!) These are hard times for families and individuals, regardless of spiritual perspective.

While the accolades pile up from previously distributed beta copies (and now, finished copies) of ***Hope Lines***, the number of people benefiting from Neil's heartfelt work continues to grow. And if YOU get value, we appreciate it if you could help spread the word, including adding a review at Amazon.com.

Sandy Dell, RScP

"Spiritual Chef Sandy"

Outreach Spiritual Practitioner & Coach

Licensed by Religious Science / Centers for Spiritual Living

https://spiritualtoolsforhungrysouls.com | ***SpiritualChefSandy@gmail.com***

ACCOLADES FOR **HOPE LINES**

"A Refreshing and Welcome New Perspective!"

As a long-time District Judge, one sees what has and HASN'T worked well in our society. In ***Hope Lines***, Neil Presley Cox's poignant examples of human discord, and his plea for a better way forward, provide a beacon of hope in a world badly in need of one.

Family life is full of challenges, and our court system should be a last resort, not the first or best place to seek answers. Better yet—as Neil suggests—find ways to avoid court entirely.

If you think (or hope) there is a better way to deal with life's problems, this book is a 'must read'. I highly recommend it, knowing you will be wiser, and better prepared, for having read it.

John Bradbury
Retired District Judge, Idaho and Clearwater counties, Idaho

"What a Wonderful Book to Help Families"

Hope Lines! What a wonderful book to help families gain the wisdom and guidance needed in today's world.

Neil Presley Cox has the experience and background, and it shows in his focus on practical solutions during these troubling times.

A must read. I highly recommend!

Gail Craig, Mother

"What People Need to Know When Raising a Family Today"

In a world where there is so much brokenness and heartache in family life, Mr. Cox's book, ***Hope Lines***, addresses the loss of common sense and lack of responsibility in society. Some have forgotten that having children is a blessing and a privilege.

I appreciate the knowledge and experiences that brought Mr. Cox to capture the essence of many a generation.

Mr. Cox speaks truth in recognizing that a firm Christian foundation backed by scripture is what people need to know when raising a family today and always. ***Hope Lines*** is well done.

Paula Kaufman, Mother of two, School district employee

"Wisdom for Today's World"

"An Impactful, Gut-wrenching Description of Life"

As an insurance adjustor, I saw tragedies and had to maintain my professionalism through painful situations. After I retired, many things I had seen bothered me.

Neil Presley Cox's book, ***Hope Lines*** is an impactful, gut-wrenching description of life when it goes off the rails. Mr. Cox offers hope and suggestion to help people get back on track. ***Hope Lines*** is well written, and Mr. Cox addresses the problems people face today with openness and compassion.

I highly recommend this book!

Russell Storey
Insurance Adjuster

"A Lawyer with a Message … and a Heart."

After meeting Neil Presley Cox in a writers' networking and critique group in Lewiston, Idaho, I fell in love with his ***Hope Lines*** manuscript. So much so, in fact, that my wife and I offered to help him publish his resource to Amazon.

Neil's 18 stories, prototypical of real life, are so well-written and engaging that ***Hope Lines*** is hard to put down. And most anyone who's suffered family strife will relate to one or more. And if you've been around awhile, you will probably see someone you know, in every single story.

While many people experiencing personal or family dissension will get value from this tome', individuals in professional roles—attorneys, counselors, ministers, coaches, and more—will also find great value.

Hope Lines is a touchstone to understanding what people in crisis are going through mentally and emotionally—a precursor to helping them. Plus, the wealth of post-story resources and "next steps" are worth their weight in personal power and relationship gold.

Neil is the perfect person to share this amazing resource. Enjoy!

Mal Dell

Elbow Grease Press

Neil Presley Cox has a way of using his personal and professional wisdom that speaks to the core of what is going on in the collective process in America.

His stories and wisdom in ***Hope Lines*** point to the path of health and healing. He speaks from where the rubber meets the road – REALITY! His wisdom is practical and can be applied to our daily lives.

Ruben Jimenez

Author, The Road Home:

A Guide for Parents with Teens or Young Adults Returning from Treatment

PREFACE: A Note from the Author

Try as you might, you cannot separate your career from your personal life. They will either weave together, like two strands of a rope, or they will intersect in a destructive crash.

I have had my share of destructive crashes. I am a criminal defense and family lawyer and this is what it's like: high-octane pain and blame games. As you will see, I found a way to truly live, to weave career, family, and faith together.

I have over twenty-five years of lawyering under my belt and in my soul. The stories in this book were born of years of working with people. So many of them, children included, were in emotional pain. Lawyers are told to be professional and detached. No one tells us how to be unemotional and clinical in the presence of a child crying for a parent she cannot have. By year two, I had long passed my quota for seeing downcast eyes on lost little ones. No longer could I stand to see children doing more of the parenting than their parents did.

Along my journey there were, of course, "coping mechanisms." Some of these were healthy and some quite the opposite. I tried to block the pain of watching bad situations by telling myself, "Children are resilient." Perhaps they can overcome growing up in a home where drug abuse is the way of life. I reminded myself that many studies say children adjust well to divorce over time. That kind of mantra has helped parents live with the pain of seeing their children hurting.

As I watched families disintegrate, hopelessness pervaded my own life. I began slipping down the slide that is alcoholism. I kept grinding along, telling myself to just get through today. This went on longer than I thought anyone could endure being miserable. I tried to ignore the pain in my gut as it grew and spread throughout my soul.

The great escape, alcohol, was no longer a coping mechanism. It grew into a monster consuming the good things in my life one by one. I had a simple choice: find recovery or lose everything—including my life.

Recovery saved me. However, without the blocking power of alcohol, the stress and sadness of lawyering stayed in sharp focus within me. Custody cases remained the most painful of all.

I tried to reach the hearts of other family lawyers to minimize conflict. Reactions varied:

The money chasers laughed.

The image/ego lawyers nodded their heads, pretended to agree and changed nothing.

The few who understood re-doubled their efforts to actually help people.

In other words, my efforts to reach out to the hearts of the other lawyers did not produce much success. I felt like Tom Cruise in "Jerry Maguire" after he had his awakening and everyone else thought he was losing it. A thought plagued me. Perhaps lawyers do not have hearts?

That kind of thinking led me full circle to the realization that I am only responsible for my own behavior. Allowing negative people to occupy space in my head will make me hopeless and even sick. In that condition, I will not be able to be of service to others.

I felt gratitude that the great leveler, time, had given me some insights. I began writing "***Hope Lines***" to help people, including myself.

When working with people, we lawyers are expressly allowed to discuss more than just the law. The American Bar Association Model Rule 2.1 provides that a lawyer "may refer not only to law but to other considerations such as moral, economic, social and political factors that may be relevant to the client's situation."

Some people were open to discussing their problems and learning of solutions. Many were not. They were in too much emotional pain. They simply couldn't help but blame others for their misfortunes. If that is where someone was on their journey, then I simply handled their legal problems in a more clinical and straightforward manner, doing the best I could for them. When needed, I made referrals to other professionals. I chose the professionals whom I knew truly cared about people.

My job is to focus on the clients and their families. If I want to do more than "cope" with being a lawyer, I must be truly willing to help others. If I keep trying to plant some seeds of hope and understanding, I will continue to be able to handle the challenges of being an attorney. Without alcohol.

People needed attention; eye-contact, cell phone turned-off attention. They needed to know that I wasn't in a hurry to sweep them out of my conference room and on their way. People needed help, spiritual help. They needed to be uplifted. We all do

They needed practical tools as well. Tools to help them understand where they are and where they are headed absent some change. And they needed compassion and honest information from a legal professional.

I explained to young people in trouble for the first time that court is composed of systems. Sometimes it feels like you are a machine part in an assembly line. You will come out the other side having been beaten and battered a bit. If you expect fairness or victory in the criminal justice system, you may be very disillusioned at the end.

The trick is to get out of the system and to not to re-enter the machinery in six months. I tried to point out that the best thing to do is to look at what led to entry into the justice (or family court) system. Face those problems with self-honesty and look to improve yourself. Get help where help is needed and move forward into more light and less stress clouds.

When they had a sense of humor, I would tell young people in trouble that the criminal career was not working well for them. They simply were not very good at it, and it was time to pursue new employment.

I told adults seeking a parenting plan and/or divorce that the real problem for the kids is *conflict* itself. "You don't win divorce or custody cases; you survive them and get them finished."

Then, there were the family members and friends of people in legal trouble. They were trying to hold things together. I told them how precious their efforts are. They are not alone. They are the rocks, saving children and healing broken hearts. When needed, I tried to give them tools to help sustain them. Those tools are the "***Hope Lines***."

Table of Contents

INTRODUCTION TO **HOPE LINES**: 18 STORIES OF DYSFUNCTION AND PAIN

*What is **Hope Lines** really about? What should I expect to gain from reading this book? Are there really tools I can use that will help me? Will you help me find them?*

These are questions you may be asking when you first pick up ***Hope Lines*** and flip through it. Will reading it really be worth your time? I believe the answer is yes. Let me explain a bit of why I wrote this book, what to expect, and the best way to use the resources found in ***Hope Lines***.

The absence of family, church and community in our children's lives is taking a toll. Other things are replacing those influences, including the Internet, video games, and street gangs in the larger cities. Many of us understand these problems intuitively. We just do not know what to do about them. Things just feel so overwhelming.

My world has been turned upside down, too. Take heart. I will throw you some ***Hope Lines***, and we will find resolutions using a tool I call the "Five Percent Rule." It just means that you do not have to tackle a problem all at once. Just for today, make one small improvement that you can build on tomorrow.

This is not another "self-help" book. It is a "help from outside yourself" book.

The stories speak to the pain and difficulty of modern living and how it has led some of you into hard journeys. Journeys into the justice system, into addictions, into loss of family. Of course, when one family member is stricken, the family unit itself is harmed.

In many ways, our society is faltering. People are feeling uneasy. There is a sense that something is not right. Connections of family, friends and community have broken down. It is the irony of our time. People have never in history had more ability to connect, yet it is a superficial, electronic connection. On a deeper level, isolation is increasing. At the same time, the foundations people could once rely on have eroded. Scandals and cynicism have led people to reject the institutions of church, government, and business.

Many commentators speak of our society's ills. "Slow down. Be present or 'mindful'," they say. My hope is that these stories and suggestions go even further than a call for mindfulness. I am calling for heartfulness. Take a breath and receive heart-based information, new information based on love.

It is a simple choice, really. Sit back and reside in a smug, intellectual cocoon. Or get going with something new. There are things outside of your usual mode of thinking that can turn your life around. Call it simply a new way of doing things or perhaps something more: Spirituality, Higher Power, God, or the Spirit of the Universe. The name we place on a change for the better is not nearly as important as the actions we take. Millions of people are finding help for their sense of loss and separation. I hope you will as well.

This book can help change your perspective about the choices you have. These stories tackle some of the bigger problems people are experiencing today. Please do not be alarmed if you see yourself or a loved one in a story. You probably will. Our society has shown a willingness to shine a light on things that used to be kept hush-hush. Addressing one's problem head-on is one of the most positive things a person can do.

Describing a problem is not enough. Practical solutions are needed. At the end of each story are suggestions to help untangle and heal the broken or frayed ropes that our lives and relationships have become. Be sure to read the calls for new hope at the end of each section.

I hope this book demonstrates that our messes are not as complex as we make them out to be. As I mentioned earlier, you don't need to solve everything at once. Do not give up when setbacks occur. Just break things down, and work on one piece of the puzzle at a time. After all, relationships, addiction, family court, and other challenges took place over the course of years. They cannot be repaired in a week. An insistence on immediate complete fixes is part of an unhealthy cycle that nourishes the problem and not the solution.

The answers suggested here are only the tip of the iceberg. Let's start the journey and tap into solutions one problem at a time and one step at a time. All you need is a key to unlock new doors. Willingness will be that key. Once you get started, momentum will help you along. Momentum is God's forward gravity. Hopelessness will be replaced by new strength and faith.

THE 18 STORY SUMMARIES

(Is your story here?)

Story1: Gray Skies Over Dad

A loving father with a serious alcohol problem, discovers the angst of marital separation from an angry, fed-up wife. Under the cloud of impending divorce, he and his two boys each exhibit the pain of limited contact differently, while the cloud of permanent family separation (i.e., divorce) looms.

Story 2: Relocation of the Heart

(To see this same story from the child's perspective, refer to "Far Away!")

The non-custodial mother of a boy is served with relocation papers by the father, who intends to move away with the child for a new job. She and two sets of grandparents would be left with little direct contact, so she fights the order. Due to state law and an indifferent judge, the relocation order is granted. As the cash-strapped mother tries to maintain a long-distance relationship, things unravel. The boy is angry and unhappy living with an increasingly abusive and absent father, but subsequent efforts to bring him back are thwarted by the legal system. The mother remarries and starts another family, but a hole remains in her heart.

Story 3: Far Away

(To see this same story from the mother's perspective, refer to "Relocation of the Heart" story.)

Ripped from the love and affection of his mother and both sets of grandparents to relocate for his custodial father's new job, things only get worse. After his increasingly distant father fails in his employment and changes jobs (again), the angry grade-schooler becomes a latchkey kid. With too much time on his hands, he starts hanging with the wrong crowd.

Story 4: Visitation Blockers

A couple—each crazy about their two young children—argue viciously for months. After he moves out and refuses to discuss the situation except to see the kids, she gives up, and files for divorce. Bitter, she also makes false allegations about abuse, which leads to a restraining order under which he can't see his kids. Then, under a temporary court order, the husband—on a very limited income, is saddled with alimony, child support, a costly psych evaluation, an expensive 16-hour domestic abuse class, and can see his kids only during paid supervised visits, at $55/hour. "Father's rights" organizations provide no direct assistance, just information. Lack of funds make it nearly impossible to see his kids. The next court date is two months away.

Story 5: Leaving Your Spouse

For years, a man puts work ahead of his wife and little girl. After each workday, the golf and drinking expand as he gets home later and later to a frustrated spouse. Eventually he meets a woman in a bar, forms an emotional attachment, and gets home really late. As the marriage spirals down a slow, indifferent death, the wife starts to reciprocate his attitudes and behaviors.

Story 6: Baby Mommas and Baby Daddies

An irresponsible, unemployed, 20-year-old, is living with his parents, and smoking pot with his buddy at every opportunity. After the prosecuting attorney's office requires a DNA paternity test, he finds out he has a baby son. He already has

3-year-old he never sees. His mom, and the baby's mom and her parents, have a very awkward sit down where little is accomplished, and harsh words are spoken. Legal action is threatened and taken on both sides, about his visitation rights. He could care less, but his mother does care. He fails to show up for the court date addressing his parental rights.

Story 7: Step-Out Parenting

Two divorced parents, each with custody of a second-grade daughter, develop a relationship. After a time, they hold a 'meet and greet', and announce to the girls, including plans to co-purchase a house and everyone move in together. The war of acceptance begins, with both girls feeling out of place, angry, and refusing to accept the situation. One wants to go live with her non-custodial parent. Both parents/step-parents are at the end of their rope with escalating conflicts. A glimmer of hope ensues.

Story 8: Jail House Dad

In jail again on drug possession charges, a dysfunctional young adult male spirals into a world of self-pity. His hyperactive, addict cell mate is going through withdrawal and scares him. Responsible for siring five or more kids with multiple mothers, he is also in held in contempt for failure to make child support payments. He demands his lawyer enforce his parental rights, even though he almost never sees any of kids. Are you (or your daughter) going to be his next "baby mamma"?

Story 9: Rock of Stability

An older couple starting retirement, is contacted by Child Protective Services to see if they can provide temporary care for their two young grandchildren. Their son is in jail for drug possession (and his wife is missing), but he calls to demands money from them for a lawyer. Again. Tired of paying for his long history of legal skirmishes, the parents refuse to help financially. They then start the process of scaling back retirement, to become full-time parents to their beloved grandkids.

Story 10: Functional

A hardworking, alcoholic man with a wife, two little girls, and a steady home services job, deals with the growing monster inside him. Drinking after work grows to hiding six-packs in the work truck, then to stops at a bar between service calls. After-breakfast shots from a bottle of bourbon stored in his garage, are next. Customers begin to complain about alcohol on his breath, and tardiness for appointments. His bosses investigate and he is fired. His marriage is cold, and uncommunicative.

Story 11: Prescription for Abuse

A recently separated wife and mother with custody of two boys, is overcome with an Oxy addiction. Bill collectors call constantly, exacerbating her stress and leading to more pills. The Oxy takes over, and she begins buying on the street when she can't get a refill. Sleeping 20 hours a day, with memory blackouts, her sons voice concern, and the situation leads to custody legal action with their father. She overdoses.

Story 12: Drug Court

Two male cousins grow up together and are still best friends as adults. Not surprisingly, when one ends up in drug court, the other is right there with him. One follows the program and graduates, experiencing pride of accomplishment, and a new life. Unfortunately, the other cousin never takes things seriously, continues to use, and lives a life of excuses and victim mentality. A judge refuses his reinstatement into the drug court program, and he is incarcerated.

Story 13: The First High

Fourth grade boys begin experimenting with energy drinks, a result of media marketing to children and associated peer pressure. One father's reliance on nightly beers reinforces the behavior, and mentally pre-programs his son for a life with regular alcohol use and abuse.

Story 14: Video Violence

A 14-year-old becomes addicted to violent video games, and posters his entire room with dark, violent graphics. His concerned mother finds some of his writings which include more ugly, violent thoughts and threats. She visits a counselor to get information and receives some grave advice. She forces a sit-down session with her disconnected son about what is going on.

Story 15: Abuser Joe

A ten-year-old boy listens to his dad screaming and beating his mom in their bedroom. Again. The noise wakes up his little brother, 3, and he tries to comfort him, taking him outside to avoid the noise. Mom comes out and drives them to his grandparents. A few days later, it happens again, worse this time. He tried to intervene but is thrown against the wall. The father leaves and cops arrive. With a swollen eye and many other bruises, the wife desperately pleads with the police not to arrest her husband.

Story 16: Domestically Non-Violent

A couple gets into a heated argument about money. She decides to go for drive, but he stops her from closing the car door. She pushes against him, but finally gives up, and they go back inside. A busy-body neighbor calls the police, and an overzealous cop arrests her for assault. The prosecuting attorney threatens a jury trial unless she pleads guilty. She signs the paperwork and pays a fine. Later, she is turned down for opportunities because of her inappropriate criminal record.

Story 17: Anxiety

A female high school graduate living at home experiences dread about next steps in her life. She lives on her phone, where she depends on feedback from her best friend, via text messages. Meanwhile, her parents give her an ultimatum: *Go to college, move out, or start paying for rent and all your personal expenses.* She is freaked, living in a mental cave of her own making, and afraid of ANY life changing decisions. Her low-paying job at a fast-food restaurant is not enough to live on her own and would barely cover rent and expenses if she stays. With low self-esteem she is terrified of college. A feeling of hopelessness keeps her frozen, with little chance of forward progress.

Story 18: Falling Through the Cracks

A teenager starts exhibiting signs of serious mental illness early in high school. Soon, in spite of his mother's best efforts, he becomes homeless with a disjointed mental capacity. To find enough to eat and warm places to sleep, he often commits illegal acts for survival, without meaning to hurt anyone. Bouncing back and forth between legal and mental health systems, he becomes an ongoing burden. His mother became a tireless crusader for his condition and situation, to no avail. He now faces significant jail time.

INTRODUCTION TO PART I: CUSTODY BATTLES AND THE SCARS OF WAR

Divorce and custody battles are afflicting families at an alarming rate. According to the magazine "Divorce.com" (yes there is such a magazine), in 2017 there were 787,251 divorces and annulments in the U.S. (December 7, 2018; Copyright 2019 Divorce Marketing Group & Segue Esprit). In 2015, one-fourth of American children under eighteen-years-old lived with a single parent. (Pew Research Center, Social and Demographic Trends, December 17, 2015).

When your family and your whole life end up in the family court system, you may feel like all is lost. Nothing will ever be right again. You may walk through stages of disbelief, hopelessness, anger, and revenge.

The machinery grinds and clangs. It pushes you along. If you try to slow things down or change a process, the machines will bludgeon you. At the end of the conveyor belt, you will feel tired, beaten-up, and defeated. Yet, this loss and disruption is the consequence of divorce and custody battles. These things birth many painful situations.

The stories in this section paint a picture of family court situations that you or other loved ones might have experienced or currently be experiencing. Are you a dad dealing with the personal pain of loss of your familial structure? Perhaps you've been tied up in an ongoing custody and visitation rights battle or you are suffering from the shock of a spouse moving a child far away from you. The stories are based on these realities. They are meant to help you walk through them with a fresh viewpoint of hope.

Whatever your particular conflict is, it will bring you consequences (e.g. pain, legal trouble), but with help comes hope. Hope leads to resolution. Let's say that again:

Conflict causes
Consequences that require
Help, which brings
Hope that leads to
Resolution!

If you are currently stuck in a court "system," please do not lose heart. The trick is to work your way through the system without becoming so frustrated and bitter that you either give up, or overreact and do something that harms your position.

Two of the four stories in this section are about a custodial parent's relocation (move) of a child and how the courts address this situation. These moves cause harm to children, because they deprive a child of regular contact with a parent. I have seen the suffering as well as the aftermath. All too often, courts approve the move without realizing the long-term harm it will cause a child. The judge and lawyers will be long gone by the time the effects are visible.

Consider the saying, "long distance relationships don't work." This phrase needs to be given new life in the context of relocation.

The effects of our actions on children can be difficult to measure, but rest assured they are long-term. What we do matters! Divorce and absent parents hurt children in a multitude of ways. One study found that divorce impacts children at unpredictable stages of their lives and that academic recovery from those impacts can lag over years. "Consequences of Parental Divorce for Child Development." Kim, Hyun Sik, (American Sociological Review, Vol. 76, Number 3, June, 2011).

Be sure to take advantage of the concrete resources offered at the end of this section.

GRAY SKIES OVER DAD:

A Loving Father Under Alcohol's Control

"The righteous lead blameless lives; blessed are their children after them." Proverbs 20:7 (NIV)

Sunday afternoon. The park is almost empty; the monkey bars are dripping wet. The sky is gray and misty, but the rain has stopped. Brent, a tired, gray-bearded man in his early thirties, swings his Ford F-150 into a parking spot. He shuts off the engine and sits, watching his two little boys step onto the soggy playground.

Isaiah, seven, runs ahead, but his younger brother, Dakota, lingers near the pickup. The kindergartener's freckled face lights up in anticipation of being chased around the toys by his father. Brent continues to sit in the driver's seat. He is looking at his cell phone, but not texting anyone.

"Come on Dad . . . you don't need your phone," yells Dakota.

Glancing at the time, Brent's face sags. He rubs at the knot in his lower gut as he realizes the boys are due home in less than an hour. *I'm going to enjoy this last bit of time. It's so ridiculous that I'll only see them six hours over the next twelve days.* His insides feel as tainted as the overcast sky.

We used to be together all the time. Brent's mind races with memories. The boys roasting marshmallows at a cabin by Lake Tahoe. Lighting a candle during a power outage. He can hear Sandy chewing him out for having a few beers at a bar after work. *I only stayed out 'til midnight a few times.*

The other times she almost ended it, Brent had persuaded her to change her mind for the sake of the children. Once, he even kept his tired promise not to drink. They went to a couple of marriage counseling sessions. After two hard weeks of sobriety, Brent came home late one night reeking of alcohol. Their fight was nasty.

Sandy's eyes bulged with anger as she screamed repeatedly, "Leave. I am through with you and your B.S. Get out!"

He yelled a few choice words back and walked into the kitchen.

As he leaned against the sink and looked outside, Brent saw the lights of a police car approaching the house. He turned back toward Sandy. "That's just great. Our gossipy neighbor called the police. Are you happy now?"

Swallowing his anger, Brent stepped onto the front porch. "Nothing's wrong, officer; we were just arguing like couples do sometimes."

Another officer questioned Sandy separately. Fortunately for Brent, she was honest. "We argued, officer. He didn't hit me or anything." The officer questioning Sandy glared at Brent with obvious hostility. He looked closely at Sandy's arms, hands, and face for signs of injury.

Brent was fortunate, and he knew it. After the officer left, he apologized and tried to be warm and apologetic with her. He wanted to make love and make up. Sandy would not look at him and retreated to their bedroom, locking the door.

The day after their dispute, Brent received another visit from a uniform. This time it occurred at the front office of the lumberyard where he worked. Brent raged inwardly as he glanced at a court order of protection. The officer explained that he was not to go to Sandy's residence and that he must avoid all contact with her and the children until court. Brent shoved the papers into his coat pocket and returned to work.

Sandy's determination this time was baffling. Brent wasn't even allowed to speak to her. *This is a real trap,* he thought. *How am I to get her back if we can't communicate?*

Reading Sandy's divorce and restraining order papers made Brent's stomach churn with fear and stress. *Wow, she even hired a lawyer. Her mom must have fronted her the money.*

Brent shook his head angrily as he read. The papers accused him of threatening to take the children and leave the country.

In court a week later, Brent told the judge that he had never said such a thing. This was half true; Brent had once stated, in a moment of great anger, he was going to take the children away from her.

The protection order was dismissed. The judge, an overweight, tired-looking man, had harsh words for both parents. "I won't be around long enough to see your children in juvenile court if you keep this up, but the next judge certainly will." Brent noticed with satisfaction that the judge was looking at Sandy as he spoke.

At the park, Brent's reverie is broken by a yell:

"Come on Dad, chase us! Play the monster game." Brent roars a monster growl at Dakota and climbs after him. He can still catch Dakota, but Isaiah can swing around and through the bars much too quickly to be caught.

Brent pulls the troops together. Isaiah refuses to leave until he hears a stern tone of voice from his father. The three of them are soaked and cold. The mood in the truck has quickly turned somber as Brent pulls away from the playground. He dreads the angry words he will hear from Sandy about his "poor choices." *How stupid are the experts who say parents need to communicate. Silence is the best policy for me.* Brent's thoughts drift into a hazy frustration at the whole world.

"Can we get an ice cream like last time, Daddy?" Dakota asks. Brent remembers Sandy's scorning words two Sundays ago. *Thanks for giving them sugar right before dinner.* He mock punches Dakota's shoulder. "No, we better get ya to Mom's, kiddo."

Brent parks in the driveway, in what used to be "his" parking spot at the family home. He can feel a tightness in his heart. Brent gives the boys a squeezing group hug. Isaiah pulls away without emotion and quickly walks into the house as his brother begins bawling. First come the tears, then a yell. "No, I'm not going Daddy. I'm staying with you!" Brent carries the squirming boy up the steps to the front door. Dakota will not let go of his dad. Suddenly, the front door opens and Sandy glares at the scene. She grabs Dakota and pulls him away from his father's pant leg. The front door slams.

Brent's emotions swirl and tear at him as he fires up the pickup truck. As always, his V-8 engine is at full roar in front of Sandy's home. He spies a loose deck rail as he drives away. He laughs out loud, a mocking laugh of small victory. Apparently, Sandy's boyfriend can't cut it as a "honey-do" man around the house.

Brent swings his pickup around a pothole at the Spuds and Suds market near his apartment. He parks and then sits a minute before entering the store. *This is my pattern, drop the kids off, then a beer run*. Arriving home, he steps over a pile of clothes just inside the door; not even a dog is there to give the place any warmth. Brent doesn't realize it yet, but his favorite watering hole is already more of a home to him than the apartment. Often, he doesn't get home from the bar until after midnight.

Brent throws some clothes off his chair and opens one of the two 24-ounce cans he brought home. Within seconds he is scrolling through pictures of women on Match.com. One prospect looks appealing: a thirty-something divorcee who describes herself as *"warm and passionate."* He finishes the beer. Rain pounds the roof as he types his selfie description: *"A fun- loving and free-spirited younger man."* Maybe she will reply.

REFLECT...

Are you hurting under gray skies right now? Do you look at your child and feel sadness and guilt instead of joy? The loneliness of not seeing your child can be unbearable.

Now you can take some time to think about everything that's happened and then do something about it. Just imagine how awesome it will be to get some relief from the heavy weight that saddens you.

Do you have any belief that your life can get better? You will need at least a pinch of such belief and willingness to try some things you might not have tried before. Try to be optimistic! It will take time. You will be very glad you made the effort.

"Conflict with your ex is harmful to your child. Therefore, please consider litigation only after exhausting other alternatives."

Here are some ideas to get started.

APPLY...

- Fight the loneliness!

Loneliness leads to hopelessness and unhealthy coping behaviors.

Spend time with emotionally healthy people in your life. Volunteer for a good cause. Attend church or a support group.

- Spend every available moment with your child.

Make this a priority. It will benefit you and your child.

Be grateful for the time you get to spend with your little one(s).

Talk to other family members about getting more time. Many of them have your child's best interest in their heart. See if they can help you.

- Find ways to reduce your ex's frustration about you.

Remember the goal is to improve your child's life and yours!

There is no "winning" or "losing" here. Clean up your side of the street as best you can.

- Ask the other parent for more time with your child.

Before taking this step, consider the best kind of approach
and be selective about timing.

You have nothing to lose in asking for more visitation time. Even an additional two-hour visit once a week will help to shorten the time between your visitation weekends.

- Take advantage of school/after-school activities.

Be upfront with your ex about such contacts.

Involvement at your child's school may provide good opportunities for more contact. Most schools are very welcoming of parents who volunteer. Let your ex know of your intentions. If you do not inform your ex, then he or she is more likely to oppose your plan.

- Consider court action.

Conflict with your ex is harmful to your child.

Therefore, please consider litigation only after exhausting other alternatives.

- Ask the court to order the "right of first refusal" for daycare.

This can be a "win-win" situation for you and your ex.

Some parenting plans require the parent having custody to offer the other parent the first option of child care instead of babysitters or daycare, when the custodial parent is at work. If your parenting plan does not have such a provision, perhaps it could be added. After all, you are saving the other parent a lot of money spent on daycare.

RESOURCE TOOLBOX

- Neuman, M. Gary, 1998 Helping Your Kids Cope with Divorce the Sandcastles Way, (Random House).

RELOCATION OF THE HEART:

The Mother's Perspective on Child Relocation

"Let us not become weary in doing good, for at the proper time we will reap a harvest if we do not give up." Galatians 6:9 (NIV)

Denise Betts answered her door to find a well-dressed man standing on her porch. He quickly handed her a small stack of papers.

"What's this about?" Denise yelled.

The process server turned to walk out of the yard. She saw the words 'Notice of Relocation' and a rush of anxiety flooded into her. Denise sobbed as she called her mother.

"Mom, please come over here right away. Jeremy's gonna move Jimmy hundreds of miles away, and I will hardly ever see him!"

Five minutes later, Denise saw her mother's yellow Ford Fiesta pull into the driveway. They sat together at the kitchen table. The relocation papers were scattered in front of them. Denise was sobbing, and her words spilled out between deep breaths. "I know Jeremy has a little over half of the parent time, but things have been going great. How can he do this? Jimmy's only seven. Why did I ever agree to that schedule? Wait until you read this garbage." Together, they read the Declaration of Jeremy Betts:

"The court should approve my move to St. Louis, Missouri. My son will benefit from the great career opportunity I have with my company there. I will be promoted to a management-in-training position. I will receive an immediate $1,100.00 per month pay raise. Besides, if I do not take the position, I will remain locked into the assembly division at the Minneapolis facility with limited chances to advance in the company. The elementary school Jimmy will attend has scored consistently high on standardized testing. As a result, my son's education will benefit from the move. My ex-wife will have extra time in the summer with our child as well as a week during Christmastime and spring break. "

They were both crying now, and Louise wrapped her arms around Denise. "I know, I know, hon. Let's see what we can do about this. The judge may not go along with it. After all, Jimmy doesn't even have family or friends in Missouri."

Denise barely heard her. "No, Mom. I just know Jeremy and Jimmy will be allowed to move. I have a bad feeling about this."

"Let's go see the lawyer your cousin always raved about."

Denise nodded her head, but her eyes were misty and dull. Louise called the lawyer's office.

After the call, Louise tried to encourage Denise. "See? They were able to get us the appointment fast. It's this Friday."

Denise's eyes finally registered hope. "But I don't know how much money it's going to cost, Mom."

The visit to the lawyer started off well. Denise and Louise really liked her; she was down to earth and sympathetic.

The lawyer told them, "I cannot guarantee you that we will succeed in blocking the move, but I can sure help give you a fighting chance." Then came the price tag: a $2,500.00 retainer.

They talked in the lawyer's parking lot afterwards. Denise was angry. "I don't have any money. How can my child's best interest come down to money? How in the world am I supposed to protect Jimmy?" She looked at her mother hopefully, almost expectantly.

Louise had to repeat herself twice. "You know I'm on a fixed income. I don't have the money to give you. I wish I did."

A few days later, Denise picked up Jimmy from his father's home. She couldn't help it; the questions poured out of her.

"So, what do you think about your dad's idea of moving to Missouri?"

Jimmy's eyes blurred teary. "I don't want to move, Mom. Do I have to?"

"I don't know yet, hon. We'll see. Have you told your father how you feel?"

"Yeah, but Dad says we have to move."

The week leading to court was a blur of fear and depression for Denise. She wrote a statement and prepared to read it to the judge, although she was not sure she would not be able to speak without breaking down in court.

On the morning of the hearing, Louise came over for support. As Denise drove them to court, she was surprised to find she was not as afraid and lost as she had expected to be. She took her seat alone at one of the two tables facing the judge's bench. Jeremy and his confident appearing attorney sat at the table to the right. When she was called to voice her side, she looked right at the judge and spoke with heart and conviction.

"Jimmy regularly spends time with two sets of grandparents here, not to mention his time with me. He has a host of friends and cousins with whom he is very close. You will be hurting him if you do this. To allow this move would be a big mistake."

Jeremy's lawyer, Mr. Cambridge, read the Minnesota law regarding relocation. Twice he pointed out that the court must presume that the move should be granted. Then he quoted from Jeremy's declaration.

The judge paused to put on his glasses. He glanced at a law book on the bench and looked at Jeremy, then Denise. "I cannot block the custodial parent's relocation, ma'am," he said evenly. "The father has made a showing of economic necessity, and I am allowing this move."

Denise's face slumped forward. Numbness nearing blackness swam inside her head. She did not hear the judge throw her a few cookie crumbs of extra time during the summers. She shuffled out of the courtroom, not to be consoled by her mother or anyone else.

Lawyer Cambridge moved on to his next case, as did the judge. Neither was troubled with thoughts about Jimmy's future.

Denise called Jimmy every night at first. Then, it became three or four times a week. She tried Skype calls with Jimmy; that lasted a few months. She sent him his own cell phone so they could talk without Jeremy hollering for Jimmy to "hurry up and get off the phone."

After the first year, Denise could not afford to pay half of the airfare for Jimmy's summer and Christmas time travel. Summers meant more time, so she gave up Christmases with Jimmy.

Long distance relationships don't work. The thought plagued Denise; it whittled away at her hope and optimism. The close bond they enjoyed was floating away like steam. She feared it would never return.

During her time with Jimmy, she noticed he was becoming sullen and withdrawn.

A couple of years after the move, Jimmy let it slip out during a phone call that his dad had changed jobs. "Dad guards people at prisons now, Mom."

Denise was startled. "When did he stop working at the factory?"

"I don't know, a couple months ago I guess. I wasn't supposed to tell you. Guess what, I got a new PlayStation, Mom."

"Nice, hon. Do you get to play a lot?"

"Yes, every day after school."

Denise tensed. "Does your dad leave you alone at home?"

"Sometimes, Mom, but I just play games 'til he comes home."

"Oh." Denise changed the subject and quickly ended the conversation. Her heart hurt, and her mind needed time to process the distressing information.

It was all too much. Denise swallowed her pride and borrowed money from a friend to hire the lawyer she and her mother had visited. She filed a modification, asking the court to return Jimmy to his mother's care. It was too late. Lawyer

Cambridge wrote a nicely worded objection and legal brief. Denise's request to modify was denied by the court for "lack of adequate cause." At least that was what the written order stated. Denise was not even allowed a court hearing on her request. Reading the order, she voiced her thoughts out loud.

"Maybe it's good I didn't have to go to court. I would have given the judge a piece of my mind about his 'adequate cause'. My nine-year-old is a latchkey kid."

The years passed. Denise remarried and had a baby girl. Her husband was a kind and supportive man. Yet, nothing could replace the hole in her heart. Jimmy was in that heart and had been forever. Worry and guilt flowed through her in patterned strands, like ribbons. *I should have hired that lawyer in the beginning. I should have done more. And how strange it is to feel guilty that I have finally found someone to share my life with.*

On a late spring day in St. Louis, Jimmy had become Jim. He was playing a zombie apocalypse game on his Apple iPod. He looked older than his twelve years. He heard his father come in from work.

Jeremy pointed to a mess of dishes in the kitchen. He roared, "Jim! Get off the waste-of-time iPod and come over here! And get that scowl off your face."

Jim immediately went to his dad, but his face wore a sullen, defiant expression.

Jeremy looked at his son. "So, tell me what time you got home after school. It's obvious you haven't done any of your chores around here."

"I was tired, Dad. Gimme a break."

This made Jeremy angrier, but Jim was already walking away.

"You're not too big for me to throw you on the ground and wallop you!" yelled Jeremy.

As he retreated to his room, Jim yelled back at the same volume, "Just leave me alone."

He slammed his door and shut out his father, shut out everything, with headphones blaring profanity-laced rap music.

Later that night, Jim called his mother; "I want to live with you, Mom. Everything is messed up here, especially Dad."

"I wish it could be, Jimmy, but unless your father agrees, it's not going to happen anytime soon. I will talk to him and see what we can do." Her voice registered false optimism. She knew there wasn't a flicker of a chance Jeremy would agree to a change of placement.

The call with Jeremy lasted about two minutes. As she expected, he quickly became angry at the suggestion that placement be changed. By the end of the call, he was roaring into the phone. "You don't have a clue what his life is like here. It's not appropriate for you to try to poison Jim against me!"

She ended the call and slumped, defeated, into a chair. Then, after a moment, she roused herself. Jeremy's tirade had not diminished Denise's motherly resolve and strength. *I'm going to try the Skype thing again. Maybe I can find a youth pastor in Omaha and get Jimmy in touch with him somehow.* She googled St. Louis churches.

REFLECT...

It really hurts. When your child isn't okay or isn't home with you, things feel terrible. You worry about the things that are influencing your child. Please take a moment and think about some of the good things in your life and in your child's life. Some of those good things are there because of you. Love is never wasted.

Can you believe, even for a moment, that things will get better? The victories may seem small in the beginning. Take joy in a small improvement and then let momentum help you along to more progress. I call this the "Five Percent Rule." It means not tackling everything at once, because it is too overwhelming. After a while, the victories will not seem so small.

APPLY…

- Communicate with your child on the medias she uses.

Put aside your feelings about texting, Facebook, Instagram or whatever your child likes to use. The goal is to stay connected.

Is your child on Facebook? Does he or she love texting but dislike telephone conversations? Meet your child at ground level and communicate, whether you like the means or not. You cannot help and protect your child without connection and communication.

- Try to make and maintain relationships with people in your child's life.

Your ex is probably not going to alert you to bad news. You will need sources of information to find out how your child is really doing.

Find out who your child's friends are, if possible. You might be able to make friends with one of their parents. This could turn out to be an excellent source of information and help down the road.

Communicate with your child's teachers and the front office person at his or her school. Call the counselor. Learn everything you can and make connections. Don't worry about where it is all leading or what to do at the moment. Keep collecting that information and keep trying to be as helpful as possible. Rewards will come and you may be able to do something with your information later.

NOTE: If a protection order or restraining order has been entered against you, you must follow the terms of the order to the letter. Do not try to "sidestep" or sneak around the order by contacting third parties. Consult an attorney if you have any questions about the order.

- Self-care is critical for you, whether you think so or not at this moment.

This is YOUR child and you are in this for the long haul.

Self-care is crucial for you to keep up your spirits and be in a good place for your child emotionally. No one knows what the future holds. If you are not doing well, then you will not be in position to help your child when the help is most needed. Be gentle with yourself. Do things you enjoy doing. Appreciate the loved ones in your life. Consider volunteering to help children if you have the time. Use your knowledge of the problems of relocations to help others in this situation. It will help you enormously, not to mention the kids you help.

- Try to find a way to add a visit or two each year.

Level your pride and ask for help with airfare from family members or friends.

You will feel much better if you can lessen the gaps between times with your child. Ask for help. Consider taking out a credit card with airfare rewards instead of other perks. If you can accumulate a lot of airfare mileage, you might be able to afford an additional long-distance visit.

- If you are in court, personalize your child and the situation for the judge.

It is up to you to show the court that separation from loved ones will harm or is harming your child.

Court can be a very dry and clinical place. You need to shift the judge's thinking to a more heartfelt understanding of your child's life. Show the court that allowing a relocation will break the child's bonds with people crucial to her emotional health! Hire a persuasive lawyer if possible. Introduce pictures of your child playing with her cousins and walking with her grandparents. Show the judge how happy your child is with his or her best friend. Make it clear that allowing the move will break the child's stable connections with people and therefore harm the child. Most judges have seen the movie, "It's a Wonderful Life." Give the judge a snapshot projection of the child's future without those important people.

- Ask the court to appoint a "guardian ad litem."

Your child needs someone to advocate about his or her best interests.

A "guardian ad litem" investigates a child's situation and reports back to the court. The judge does not have time to go to people's homes or to meet with children. The "G.A.L." is the eyes and ears of the judge.

You should give input into who is assigned to the role of guardian ad litem. You want someone with a real heart for children.

RESOURCE TOOLBOX

- Relocation Issues in Child Custody Cases, edited by Philip M. Stahl and Leslie M. Drozd, (The Haworth Press, Inc.). 2006.

FAR AWAY:

The Child's Perspective on "Relocation of the Heart"

"Fathers, do not exasperate your children; instead, bring them up in the training and instruction of the Lord." Ephesians 6:4 (NIV)

"I've got something exciting to tell you, Jimmy."

Jimmy looked at his dad. "Is it about the fair coming next week?"

"No. Sit down, kiddo."

Unnerved by the tone of his father's voice, Jimmy sat stiffly on the couch, nervously pulling on his shirt.

"We are going to be moving to a different city in a couple months. It'll be great! You'll meet new friends, see new stuff."

Jimmy was silent for a few seconds. Then, the words rushed out. "But I don't want to move Dad, no!" He stood up.

"I'm sorry you feel that way, but it has to happen because of my job. Don't worry about it right now, and do not say anything to your mother about it, okay?"

"Why can't I tell Mom?"

"She will be finding out tomorrow, but this is an adult thing for your mom and I to talk about."

Jimmy started doing cartwheels in the living room. Unease about the move propelled his energy.

A couple days later he waited for his mom to pick him up for the start of her three-day. When she pulled up to the curb, he forgot to hug his dad as he ran outside.

Jeremy walked outside and handed Denise a gym-sized bag. For a brief second, they glared at each other, then Jeremy walked away. Not a word had been spoken between them.

As Jimmy and his mom drove away, the words came out. “I don’t want to move, Mom.”

“So, your dad told you about it, huh?”

“Uh huh.”

“Have you told him how you feel about it?”

“Yeah. He says we have to move no matter what.” His eyes grew watery.

Denise pulled Jimmy into a tight hug. “Things will be okay, little guy,” she said, rubbing his head.

He loved it when Mom ran her fingers through his hair. Still, the hurt remained. Things were not okay.

At noon on Sunday, Jimmy was back home at his father’s. He jumped up over the good news. “We get to go to Nana’s and Papa’s–yeah!” Jimmy ran to the front door.

“Hold on, we’re not leaving until you empty the dishwasher,” his father replied.

He did his chore then went across the street to play with Mack. Mack was only in first grade, but they were great buds.

Jimmy’s paternal grandparents lived in an older house in a quiet neighborhood north of the city. Jimmy thrust halfway out of his seat when he saw two of his cousins playing with a dog in the yard. “Look, there’s Carl and his sister!” He jumped out and ran over to them.

After a while they came inside. Jimmy heard arguing and saw that his Papa’s face was red. Jimmy spoke for the kids. “Can we have something to eat, Nana? What’s the matter?”

Nana popped up from the table to grab them a snack. “Nothing, we were just having an adult discussion.”

Jeremy got up as well.

"Jimmy, we are gonna get going. Tell everyone goodbye." "But we just got here, Dad. I don't want to go."

"You heard me. Come on."

Nana gave Jimmy a hug, but her eyes were transfixed on her adult son. "Love you, Jimmy boy, we'll see you soon, okay?"

Jimmy walked sullenly to the car. He was silent for a while as they drove. Then he asked meekly, "Why did we have to leave so early, Dad?"

"Because your grandparents were arguing with me about our having to move, that's why."

"Well, I don't want us to move either, Dad."

"Knock it off! I told you we are not talking about it. It's going to happen and you might as well accept it."

Angry and sad at the same time, Jimmy laid his head against the backseat window on the way home.

A few days later at school, Mrs. Rodriguez, Jimmy's teacher, took him aside. She had noticed a shuffle in his walk as he walked into class in the mornings. He seemed down. "Jimmy, is everything okay with you? Anything you need to talk about?"

"No, not really."

"Is everything okay at home?"

"Um, yeah, but we're moving."

Mrs. Rodriguez called Jimmy's parents after school and left a message suggesting a meeting. Neither Denise nor Jeremy returned the call.

The night before court, Jimmy was at home with his father. Nervous energy filled the air. Jeremy was edgy and silent. No more than "good night" was spoken between them the whole evening.

After school the next day, the mood had completely changed. In full Disneyland dad mode, Jeremy grabbed Jimmy up into his arms. "How about we go have an ice cream?"

Two weeks later, Jimmy watched his dad and a co-worker loading their stuff into a rental truck. Childhood exuberance had replaced sadness; now he was excited over the big events. Mack came over, and they made a game of climbing in and out of the truck, until his father told him to stay out of the way of the heavy lifting. Jimmy helped bring his toys into the truck.

As they drove away in silence, Jimmy looked back at his street and the big tree in the front yard. "Goodbye tree," he said solemnly.

St. Louis was hot and muggy, but Jimmy didn't mind. Every new thing was exciting as they moved into their two-bedroom duplex.

As summer ended, Jimmy grew nervous about his new school. By his third day, the feeling had melted away. Jimmy made friends easily, and he liked his teacher.

Home was a different story. His dad was grumpy all the time, something to do with his work.

One night, Jimmy was sitting on the floor in his bedroom, playing with Legos. "Hey, Jimmy," Jeremy yelled towards the bedroom door. "Come out here; we gotta talk about something."

Jimmy walked down the hall, into the living room. "What's the matter, Dad?"

"Well, you're a big boy now, so I want you to be a man about this, okay? Jimmy's face filled with alarm. "About what, Dad?"

"I had to change jobs; I will be working at a prison an hour from here. That means you will be alone after school on some days until I get home. Maybe some Saturdays too."

"Can't I stay at a friend's house?"

"Well, that might be okay sometimes, but not most of the time."

He missed his mom, his family back home. The feelings were there, under the surface, but Jimmy kept them hidden from the world and from himself, too. TV and video games helped keep them away.

At first, Jimmy came home right after school, as he had promised his dad he would. He didn't mind, really, except for a few times when he heard strange noises in the house.

Once, when he was eight, he thought he heard "growling." The noise was repeated and Jimmy panicked and ran outside, accidentally locking the door behind him. He sat on the porch, crying until a "stranger" came over to help. He was actually a kind, elderly neighbor. After failing to get Jeremy on the phone, the man managed to open a window and let Jimmy back inside.

Bryce lived across the street from Jimmy. All summer, Jimmy had been watching Bryce play on his basketball court or run through the sprinkler. Shy anxiety kept him from crossing the street. Bryce took the initiative. A week before school was to resume, Bryce bicycled across the street. Jimmy sat on his porch playing on his iPOD.

"What game are you playing? Bryce asked.

"Zombie Wars."

In fifteen minutes they were best buds.

The boys preferred Bryce's house; he had both a PlayStation and WII system. Bryce's mom was super nice; Jimmy felt at home with her gentle kindness. She noticed his isolation and always let Jimmy come over after school.

Jimmy forgot about his grandparents and cousins, until a trip to Minnesota was at hand. Then it was like they'd never been apart. He was sad when they had to leave.

Things changed during the fourth summer following the move. Jimmy answered the phone one night and could tell something was bad. His mom was struggling to sound calm and okay.

"Jimmy, I have to tell you something. I feel so bad, but I can't afford to pay my half of your plane ticket for the summer. We will still see each other during Christmas vacation, and I will try to drive down there this summer to see you for a couple days, okay?" Her voice was almost pleading.

"It's okay, Mom." Jimmy answered flatly. He didn't respond with more than a few syllables to her efforts to get him to talk about the situation.

Bryce moved away. Jimmy found new friends. Like found like. Jimmy's friends were video gamers. They were also slightly troubled on the "sidelines" kids. Then there was Vance, sixteen, and more lost than any of them.

Jimmy had been angry with his dad so long, he'd forgotten the reasons. He was too intimidated by his father to express anger or true feelings. Sarcasm and avoidance carried the day. Jimmy stopped coming home after school until just before his father came home after six o'clock.

Jimmy had become Jim. On a muggy late September day after school, Jim was hanging out with Vance.

"Bum me a fiver, man." Jim pretended to be angry.

Vance knew when Jim got in his face, he was just asking for a cigarette rather than money. He handed him one from a pack of Camels.

The pair smoked behind a dumpster in an alley near Jimmy's junior high school. Neither was in a hurry.

Leaving the alley, the two of them wandered along a busy street of strip malls and convenience stores in the suburbs of St. Louis.

"Ya wanna go to Gameplay?" asked Jim.

Vance shook his head. "What's the point without any money? …But I know a guy who's got some bud!" Their steps quickened.

They walked up cracked cement steps to a run-down house. The front door was open, and they knocked on it hesitantly. A man's voice from somewhere inside yelled, "What'cha want?"

Vance tried to make his voice sound deep and confident, but it cracked. "We're looking for Dale," he says. A moment passed, then a teenager in dreadlocks came outside.

Dale glared at Vance. "You shouldn't have come here, chowder. And who's this?" He wagged a dismissive finger at Jim.

Vance tried to smooth things. "No worries, he's my friend."

Dale came right to the point. "Well, what are ya wanting?"

"We don't' have any money; we were just hoping to get high."

Dale looked at them sympathetically. "Sorry, man, no can do." He walked inside the house, shutting the door on them.

Vance and Jim walked around town aimlessly for a while. As they parted, Vance said, "Jim, come up with twenty bucks tomorrow and we'll hook up, okay?"

He nodded in agreement, but he had no idea how to get any money.

Jim made it home just a few minutes ahead of his father. He grabbed a bag of chips from the kitchen and glanced at the pile of dishes. He knew trouble was coming, but there was no time to do anything about it now. As he went into his room, he heard the front door open.

REFLECT…

It hurts to actually see what some of your grownup decisions can produce for the kids. Do you ever think that the hurt is God's way and nature's way of steering us in the right direction? Do you think your hurt could actually help your children by leading to better things?

"Put the brakes on your life just for a bit. Take some time and think about your life and your decisions."

Put the brakes on your life just for a bit. Take some time and think about your life and your decisions. This is a chance to make things better – much better! You can help your child and feel good on the inside all at the same time.

APPLY…

- Examine your priorities.

When making big decisions, how much thought do you really give to your child's long-term emotional needs?

The courts have developed a well-known standard to decide matters involving children. It is called the "best interest of the child." For us parents, this standard should be the number one criterion when we are considering big changes in our lives. Please, take some time to reflect upon your child's future. Are you living on the basis of your wants, or on your family's needs?

- If you are considering relocation with a child, ask your child's close relatives, friends, and teachers what they think about the idea.

Keep your mind open to input!

When you want to start a new relationship or move your family, you want it more than anything. You naturally look for allies who will support your decision. Swallow your pride and find out what other people in your child's life think about your plans.

- Communicate with your child in different ways about what is happening.

Mention your idea and then listen!

This holds true for more than just proposed moves. If you listen to your child at different times in his or her life, you may be surprised. Perhaps just once, your child will start to open up about things. Practice listening without trying to sell your opinion! Not only will you learn about what he or she thinks, you will find clues to what is best for your child.

- Keep lines of communication open with your ex and with the child's extended family.

Put aside your frustration for your child's sake!

This may be the hardest thing to do in a custody situation. It may also be the most important. Conflict between a child's most treasured adults is very harmful.

RESOURCE TOOLBOX

- Royko, Dr. David, 1999, Voices of Children in Divorce, (St. Martin's Griffin).

VISITATION BLOCKERS:

Bitter Spouse Destroys the Life of Divorcing Spouse

"Have I not commanded you? Be strong and courageous. Do not be afraid; do not be discouraged, for the Lord your God will be with you wherever you go." Joshua 1:9 (NIV)

There's got to be some group that can stand up for guys like me. Bodee googles "fathers' rights." Law firms with pro-father slogans, appear on the screen. There are a couple of nonprofit groups as well.

A call center rep replies to Bodee's questions. "We can provide you with a compact disc loaded with information, including contact info for other groups. Or we can mail the information to you." Frustration mounts; Bodee feels his face flush.

"I don't need a compact disc. I need someone to go to bat for me with this judge that's not lettin' me see my kids! There's no reason for what's happening to me."

"I'm sorry sir, we do not provide an attorney or advocate for your court case." Click.

How had it come to this mess? Bodee debates again whether to call his lawyer. The last time they met, the guy couldn't remember the names of Bodee's children. "Their names are Lucas and Josie, three and six," he had stated emphatically.

It'll just be the paralegal on the phone, and I'm not in the mood to see another forty-dollar charge for a phone call. Indecision wins out as Bodee surfs the Internet mindlessly.

Bodee and Astanah Betts had been miserable. Every conversation was an argument. Bodee's approach was to avoid talking. Astanah became a yeller.

Bodee couldn't stand to listen to her anymore. He moved into his fifth wheel on his friend and co-worker Mark's property. Astanah and he talked for hours those first few days. His sadness was nothing compared to hers; she cried constantly and begged him to come back.

Bodee's mood changed on the third day. She'd texted him over twenty times, trying to get him to talk. He decided to stop talking to her, except to ask to see the kids. "Can I have the kids after work until Sunday?" he typed.

"Come over after work and we'll talk," she replied.

Bodee knew what that meant, but he did not want to anger her. "Ok, but I have plans for the kids, so I can't stay long."

He knocked on what was now her door, fearful their conversation would explode into anger. Josie opened the door and jumped into his arms. "What are we going to do, Daddy?"

"You'll see, sweetie. Let me talk to your mom a minute."

Astanah started to embrace him, but Bodee pulled away from his wife's hug. "Listen, I want us to be friends, but that's it. I know this is hard. I am very afraid you're going to get mad and stop letting the kids stay with me."

"You know I would never keep the kids from you," she said. Astanah believed it was true, at that moment.

And so went their pattern for weeks: Astanah insisting on seeing him, and Bodee trying to set her down gently.

Astanah's friend Lucy had a friend who was a paralegal. She drafted paperwork and filed for divorce. She held off filing a proposed schedule for the children. A few weeks went by without any problems. Even the children seemed to be doing okay with the new situation.

One evening, Astanah had just put the kids to bed. She was lounging on the couch when her phone beeped a warning that she had a text message from Lucy.

"So, Bodee's already seeing someone? What do you know about her?"

Astanah bolted from the couch and dialed Lucy's number. "Alright, Lucy, tell me what you know."

"All I know is my husband told me Bodee has been going out with some young gal about nineteen," Lucy said. "I don't know her name or anything."

Alerted into action, Astanah called Bodee. She did not hear the first part of his explanation, because she was yelling too loudly. Out of breath, she stopped her tirade and listened for a moment.

Bodee defended himself angrily. "What right do you have to dictate whether I date or not?"

"We just filed the divorce case and you're dating? I thought we were going to keep each other informed about big things like this."

Bodee was in no mood to tolerate her yelling. "It's my business, and you need to stay out of it." He clicked "end" on his cellphone.

After that, Bodee's calls to Astanah went to her voice mail. He tried texting. "Can I see the kids after work today or this weekend?"

Astanah replied back quickly, "No, we are going to wait until the court hearing." After that, she did not bother replying to his texts.

She had Bodee served with restraining order papers the following day. She was asking that he have only "supervised" visitation with their children. Bodee would have to pay to see Lucas and Josie. A court hearing was scheduled for two weeks down the road.

As he read, Bodee's face reddened. His hands clenched into fists. Electric energy surged through him. *She's insane if she thinks this will fly with me. This is beyond unreasonable.*

He skimmed through a sentence ordering "Mr. Betts to pay both child support and alimony."

He whipped up a text to Astanah: "So you want all the money, and I can live in my car and not see the kids, huh?"

She ignored the text.

Several days went by. Bodee's texts asking to visit the children went unanswered. He swallowed his pride and borrowed money from his dad to hire a lawyer.

Bodee worked at the radiology department at a small hospital. During breaks, at lunch, every chance he could, Bodee talked. He couldn't help but spill out the story to anyone with a sympathetic ear. After he left these conversations, Bodee's co-workers kept the fire going.

The secretary up front could be counted on for information. Sally had opinions about everyone in the department. She told Bodee's best friend, Mark, that Bodee must have done something no one at the hospital knew about. "How else could the courts keep a good father like Bodee away from his children?"

Mark looked right into her eyes. "I know Bodee better than anyone. He's done nothing wrong. The only wrong is what's being done to him."

Sally continued to offer speculation. Before long, a rumor went around that Bodee cheated on his wife for years. When another friend reported the story to Bodee, he looked vacantly at the man with pained eyes. "I don't have the time to worry about people's gossip right now."

The morning of court, Bodee was home, nervously getting ready. He shaved and put on a suit and tie. Bodee's handsome, tanned features looked sharp in his nice clothes. But a closer inspection revealed dark circles under his eyes and a look of perpetual worry. He'd been agonizing about not seeing his kids. They probably feel like I abandoned them and don't care. The thought hurt. Fear gripped him: he was becoming a stranger to them; he would never get to see them. *I hope the judge understands what she's pulling*. He shuddered at the thought of losing in court.

Bodee's lawyer had not told him he was about to walk into a political hornet's nest. Judge Andrew Carlin had been watching events unfold in a neighboring county. An old friend of Judge Carlin's, Judge Robinson, had granted a father reasonable visitation every other weekend with his young son. The mother of that child had urged Judge Robinson to make the visitation supervised only. She claimed the father had threatened to harm her and the child. She brought no witnesses or evidence to her court hearing. Judge Robinson knew she had made the same allegations against previous boyfriends; her other attempts to get restraining orders had been denied.

The community was shocked when the mother appeared on the evening news to make a plea for public help in finding her baby. Her ex-boyfriend and the child had disappeared. An Amber Alert was issued, and everyone feared the worst when the man's car was found submerged in a local lake.

The public was mobilized against Judge Robinson. People were saying he didn't care about children, that he had denied requests for restraining orders in other cases. Family court decisions in the region were being closely watched. A year later the man and the baby were located in Florida. Mother and child were reunited.

Judge Carlin was shocked by the angry rhetoric against Judge Robinson, resolving to be careful.

In the middle of the firestorm over Judge Robinson's decision, Bodee and Astanah Betts appeared in court on her request for a temporary order and a restraining order.

Bodee's lawyer had told him he would, at minimum, get a good ruling on visitation. He was completely unprepared to hear Judge Carlin announce his decision:

"I must say there is not a lot of information here to support the mother's request for supervised visitation. Nevertheless, you have alleged that Mr. Betts made a threat against you a few months ago. To protect you and your child, I am going to err on the side of caution. I will grant your request for a restraining order. I am ordering that Mr. Betts present himself for a psychological evaluation at court services. For now, visitation will be supervised. Another hearing will be scheduled after I review the psychological evaluation to determine whether the need for supervision will continue. Also, I am ordering that Mr. Betts pay child support and alimony pending further order of the court."

As he left the courtroom, Bodee walked past his wife and two of her friends. Astanah glared at him with mean satisfaction.

A few days later, Bodee walked into his lawyer's office. "I need to see my lawyer right away."

"I'm sorry sir, Mr. Burnadetti is not available. Would you like to speak to his paralegal?"

"I guess so."

A young professional woman emerged from an office. They talked in the foyer of the office.

"What now?" Bodee asked hopefully.

"You will need to follow the court's orders to the letter. Make your appointment for the psych eval right away. And here is a list of professional visitation supervisors."

As Bodee looked at approved supervisors, his face grew taut. "Are you kidding me? The cheapest one charges $55.00 per hour. How am I supposed to afford that, along with everything else the court ordered me to pay? Does the judge expect me to live in a car for the next ten years?"

The paralegal was unmoved. "I know, but you will have to do it. If you don't regularly visit the kids, your wife will be able to argue that you are not taking advantage of visitation awarded you – that you are effectively abandoning your children."

Bodee was thoroughly depressed. "This is like something out of a nightmare. I don't know how, but I will see what I can do."

He made the appointment to begin the supervised visits and found himself in a cluttered, sparsely furnished office. The professional supervisor, a young stern-faced woman, sat across from him.

"We will need advance payment for at least two supervised visits. The visits are two hours, so we will need two hundred and twenty dollars upfront, is that OK?"

Bodee searched for a sympathetic ear. “But, what is the point of this supervising business, anyway? What do you do as supervisor?”

“I cannot tell you why the court ordered this. I was not at your hearing. As for my role, I must be present every minute you visit with the children. I will observe and write a report about how the visits progress.”

Bodee paid for four hours with his children. The first visit was scheduled for the following Friday afternoon.

On Friday, Bodee nervously entered the office and looked around for his children, who were not there. The supervisor was a middle-aged tired-looking woman. She asked him to take a seat in an adjoining office.

After a few moments, he heard Astanah and the kids talking to the woman. Stress-anger churned through him. Astanah was bad-mouthing him! He heard her warn the woman. “Watch the kids at all times, Bodee cannot be trusted.”

The supervisor gave Bodee a clipboard with forms to review and sign. Noticing his jaded look, she said “Mr. Betts, it’s in your best interest to play nice here, meaning follow the rules to the letter.”

Bodee felt defensiveness rising within him. “I’m not sure what you mean, but please don’t believe everything you hear from my ‘ex, okay?” He signed the form and followed the woman into a large play area.

Emotions surged through him as he saw Lucas and Josie for the first time in four weeks. They were sitting together, looking at him mutely and slightly afraid. This troubled Bodee for a second. Then, he ran to them and hugged them tightly. The kids paused, then returned the hug. Bodee was unaware he was crying.

The supervisor sat on a chair and watched the interaction. Despite the artificial surroundings, Bodee managed to ignore the observer and enjoy the time.

Two days after the visitation, Bodee located the court services office for his psychological evaluation. His bad mood grew worse as he read the psychologist’s “fee agreement.” When Bodee was finally escorted into Dr. Cromley’s office, he noticed the doctor had Astanah’s Declaration in his hand.

Bodee wasted no time letting his feelings be known."This is such a waste of time and money. I haven't done anything wrong."

Dr. Cromley was quick to answer. "You are angry and frustrated, I understand that. Do you understand that your wife has alleged that you committed one or more acts of domestic violence and that the court granted her a protection order?"

"I understand it, but it's all a lie."

"My role as the court-appointed psychologist is to make recommendations concerning the safety and best interest of the children. It is not my job to second guess the court's decision in this case." Dr. Cromley looked at Bodee in silence for a moment.

"Fine, do what you need to do, I guess," was all Bodee could muster as a reply.

Dr. Cromley took notes as he asked Bodee questions. Then, he handed Bodee a standardized test to take.

When they were finished, Bodee asked Dr. Cromley to get his report to the court as quickly as possible. "I cannot afford anymore supervised visit fees, and the court said it would continue until your report was done."

"Please understand that the report will not be submitted until the bill is paid for my service, Mr. Betts."

Bodee went to the well a second time and borrowed money from his dad to pay the psychologist. His dad told him, "I'll do everything I can for you, but I can't help you with money anymore."

The second visit with the children went well. Talking with the supervisor, Bodee told her he was awaiting a report from the psychologist. "After that, the visits will not need to be supervised," he said confidently. "I just do not have any money and I was wondering if we could at least schedule a visit for next week."

"I'm sorry sir, pre-payment is required."

Three weeks passed, another block of time without the kids. Bodee called his lawyer every other day to see if the psychologist's report had been received. Nothing.

He grew more and more depressed. *Another month of not getting to see my children, and no one cares.*

Bodee was at work. His cell phone buzzed with an incoming call. His lawyer's receptionist. He stepped into a hallway away from people.

"Mr. Betts, the psych report is here, and you may pick up a copy. Unfortunately, the recommendation is that supervised visitation continue until you complete a sixteen-hour domestic violence information school course. The next one is scheduled for two months away, and the fee is two hundred and twenty-five dollars."

Bodee hung up the phone. He was sweating; his insides were weak. He walked into his boss's office. "I have to go home; I am really sick," he said.

He went home and began his "father's rights" search on the Internet

REFLECT...

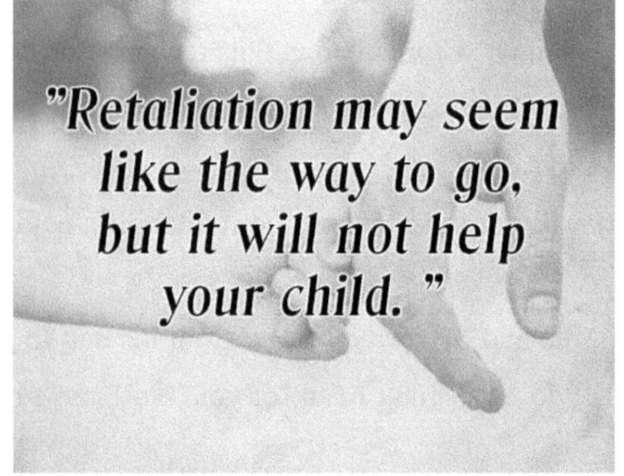

Are you frustrated and feeling like you have the right to retaliate? Your feelings are understandable. Please take some time to consider things. Retaliation may seem like the way to go, but it will not help your child.

Step away from the fire and the burning feelings for a moment. A bit of guidance from someone who has your back might help you find some direction. After that, your actions will be focused and good. For now, keep your side of the street honorable.

APPLY...

- Do not give up.

People change. Situations change. Keep doing the next right thing for your child.

It is surprising in life how situations that appear impossible often make a surprising and sudden shift for the better. Besides, when you do the right thing in the face of obstacle after obstacle, inner strength emerges. Your heart starts to feel whole. A change may take a long time. It will happen. Keep fighting for your children and your right to parent them.

- Step outside of yourself and take a broad view of things.

Try to step outside of your own perspective and frustration so you can be aware of opportunities that arise.

Opportunities float by more often than you might think. Try to be open to them. Community programs, self-help groups and kind people abound in this world. Take a look at these organizations and see if there is any assistance available for you.

Keep looking for help and be open to suggestions from trustworthy people. Ask people in the court system questions. Let go of your pride. Ask family members to help with legal fees. Ask lawyers for discounts.

- Explore fathers' rights organizations.

You might get help from one of the organizations fighting for fathers' rights.

If you are a father being denied visitation rights, explore some of the fathers' rights organizations. Some of these groups are working very hard to rectify injustices in the family court system. One of them is the American Coalition of Fathers and Children (ACFC). (www.acfc.org). You will gain access to a wealth of information and maybe, just maybe, you can get personalized help with your own situation.

Please be aware that some websites supposedly devoted to "fathers' rights" are simply advertisements from lawyers fishing for new clients. They may be excellent attorneys, but they are not public service organizations.

- Even if you tried it before, consider mediating differences with your ex.

Perhaps there is a chance to find new ground or call a truce on the court fighting.

Put aside your frustration for a moment and approach your ex or the court to see if the case can be mediated. Remember, the goals are health, love, and survival.

Winning is not part of the equation. You are trying to help your children by being with them.

Ask around for the names of good mediators. Often, the mediators in custody disputes are local attorneys. You want someone with experience and the stature (persona) to exert some influence on people.

- Get involved in helping others experiencing the same problem as you!

Being part of the solution for others in your situation will help you as well.

Fathers' rights organizations can help you, but you can also help them! It is empowering to use your experiences towards helping others with the same problem.

RESOURCE TOOLBOX

- American Coalition of Fathers and Children. (www.acfc.org).
- National Fatherhood Initiative, 20410 Observation Drive, Suite 107, Germantown, MD 20876. (fatherhood.org).
- Warshak, Dr. Richard A., 2010, Divorce Poison: How to Protect Your Family from Bad-mouthing and Brainwashing, (Harper).

A CALL FOR NEW HOPE AND FAITH

Have your life's dreams been smashed? The waves of life knock us down, and hope is hard to come by when this happens. How people turn out, how relationships go, these are in God's hands, not ours. Our job is to continue loving the people in our lives, especially the children. We keep connecting with them and offering them hope even when we are feeling crushed inside. This approach won't "fix" things. But it WILL strengthen the ties that bind us and put us on the side of the helpers instead of the destroyers.

So, the courts won't fix our problems. Sometimes the courts make them worse. Who or what can we trust? Where is a rock-solid foundation to be found, one that offers inner peace and a design for living? Millions of people have found their answers to these questions in faith. If you are sick and tired of being sick and tired, then perhaps you are ready to find something beautiful! A pinch of willingness is all it takes to begin. Do not struggle or get locked into analysis paralysis. Feel your heart's longing and start exploring for answers.

INTRODUCTION TO PART II: FAMILIES TORN APART

Many of us sense that things are not right. Often there is a feeling of not living right mixed with all the stress of modern life. The stories you are about to read examine some of the origins of those feelings. Choices we make create consequences. Infidelity is one such choice. Consider the following quote about infidelity in our society:

> "Accurate statistics on infidelity, which are hard to come by since most infidelity is secret, suggest that marital unfaithfulness is widespread. According to the Associated Press and the Journal of Marital and Family Therapy, in 41 percent of the marriages one or both spouses admit to infidelity, either physical or emotional. …{Only} about 31 percent of the marriages endure after an affair has been admitted to or discovered." (DivorceSource.com; May 2015).

Our relationships with each other and with God are causing internal strife. Yet, there is help available. Help your future by taking a few moments to decide how you would like to parent the next child that comes along. Take a look around at what is happening to children in America. Fewer and fewer fathers are living at home with their children. Custody battles are becoming the norm. Confusion, isolation, anxiety, and addiction are sweeping over the lives of young adults.

For examples, cheating on your spouse or partner poisons a relationship and usually leads to break-up. Choosing to have a baby with a person who is active in addiction and/or is uncaring towards others leads to single parenting and little support.

The heart sends quiet messages. "This is wrong." "What about the baby?" Those flickers of doubt in the heart come from the deepest part of who you are. Call it your conscience or your soul. It does not matter what you call it. It will mean everything in your life if you take a moment to process them and then talk with a trusted and caring person.

You can use the messages towards the good or you can continue to ignore them. The want roars on, blocking out the heart's messages. There is always a difficult choice today and then again tomorrow. Keep giving in to the wants and pretty soon your choices will be narrowed down to unhappy ones. Choices like: Should I hire this lawyer or that one for divorce court? Or: Do I want to see my child on Thursdays and Sundays, or Tuesdays and Saturdays?

Young people are having babies without doing any life preparation for the great responsibility that comes with parenting. They are also doing so without being in a committed relationship. Also, there are many men out there having sex with multiple partners and, thereby, having many children. A lot of them are doing so without any desire to be a father.

People are being thrust into the role of "parent" for kids not their own biological children. Step-parenting is one such situation. Also, grandparents are raising a lot of children, picking up the broken relationship pieces. They didn't plan for it, and they didn't want to do it. They do it from a place of pure love, despite exhaustion. Remember:

Conflict causes
Consequences that require
Help which brings
Hope that leads to
Resolution

Whatever choices you have made in the past, there is good news. We are all here to learn and grow towards something bigger than we once were. After each of the stories here you will find some resolutions to consider. Start your journey by using the Five Percent Rule to make a small change today. With momentum from your start, you will feel more than five percent better!

THE ENDING STARTS BEFORE THE END

Long before the end,
The ending begins.
Thoughts of brighter gardens
Across the street.
That beautiful neighbor.
The house of no problems.
Perfect distance.
Then comes the waves
of self-pity, self-this, self-that.
This is too hard. I deserve to have fun.
Comparing the half-real
With the totally false.
And all the while,
Opting out.
"Leave me alone."
My right to be happy
Explodes across the cerebral cortex.
Noisy and dominating.
I can no longer hear
the soft heartbeat
of hearth and family.
The upcoming hurt
to children and spouse,
ignored

in the quest for the outwardly beautiful.
A fire has been lit.
Now it rages unchecked,
fueled by my rights,
my wants,
my needs.
My oh my.
Small arguments are now major justifications.
It is time to start over.

If you want to enjoy more of these poems by Neil Presley Cox, for people in inspirational recovery, capture his book of recovery poetry on Amazon:

Alcoholprism

https://amzn.to/2ClaxmM

LEAVING YOUR SPOUSE:

A Marriage Spiraling Downward

"Marriage should be honored by all, and the marriage bed kept pure, for God will judge the adulterer and all the sexually immoral."

Hebrews 13:4 (NIV)

"I can't even believe what I'm hearing. You're going to throw away a marriage for some floozy you met? What about little Kimmie?"

Nick grimaced as he held the phone away from his face. He wanted to hang up.

"Mom, you don't know the whole story. Liz has been pulling some stuff with other guys. I haven't thrown anything away; I'm just trying to figure out what to do."

"Well, in your figuring, I hope you will think about Kimmie. I just can't understand any of this. Your father and I didn't raise you like this."

She kept on talking, but Nick was barely listening. He was overwhelmed by thoughts and emotions. He felt a heavy jolt of pain in his heart. For one short moment he was convicted with the truth of her words. His head visibly shook as he pushed away the feeling. He wanted his new love more than anything else. *No! I won't be talked out of this! People just don't understand. I have a right to be happy.*

His resolve to break up the family was restored. He just needed to get his mother off the phone. "All right, I will think about what you're saying, Mom. I promise."

Work had consumed Nick's life the past few years. He wasn't getting out of his office until six or seven o'clock. Usually, he'd get in a few holes of golf or stop for a few drinks before hitting the highway. Then came a forty-five-minute drive home.

Three months before the conversation with his mother, Nick was sitting in the bar at Red Robin. Seated beside him was a young woman named Sheila. The week before, he had started a friendly conversation with her. She was looking at Nick with shining eyes. Three beers in, Nick was in his element now.

"Wow, a woman treating me nice, what a rare treat!" He half jumped off his bar stool as he realized he had spoken the words out loud.

"I'm sorry, Nick, what was that?"

"Oh, I was just saying what an awesome lady you are!" She waved her beer at him and drew closer.

A few hours later Nick pulled into his driveway. It was already dark. He dreaded facing Liz inside.

She was standing her ground to meet him in the hallway. He leaned forward to kiss her, but she pulled away.

"It's almost nine o'clock, Nick. Apparently, you have zero interest in spending time with me."

"Give me a break. You don't even know what kind of day I've had."

"Maybe you should tell me what kind of night you've had. I called your office at six o'clock, and they said you had already left."

Nick tried to conceal his anger over her snooping. "Yeah, well I had a couple beers at Red Robin to unwind. Met up with a couple friends. I'm sorry I was gone longer than I planned to be."

"I'm tired of being last on your priorities list. I'm sick of it. By the way, Terri and I are going to have a girls' weekend the last weekend this month, so don't plan anything. I'm going to bed."

She walked away, ignoring his protest about the weekend.

Things were frosty between them, and it didn't get any better when Liz left for her weekend. That Sunday night, Nick was watching TV after tucking Kimmie into bed. He had tried texting Liz all weekend. She only replied once, and that was to ask how Kimmie was doing.

He heard a car pull into the driveway. Nick looked out the window and saw Terri's Honda Accord. He thought he saw a man in the backseat as his wife walked towards the house. Nick started to go outside to investigate, but the car was already motoring down the street. Liz walked past him with an annoying smirk. He smelled the booze on her.

Nick followed her down the hallway. "We need to talk."

Liz turned around and threw her arms around Nick, kissing him sloppily. "So, how was it sitting at home, waiting for me for a change?"

"Who was the guy in the backseat?"

"A friend of Terri's."

"Did you spend the whole weekend with him?"

Liz's eyes flamed. She was relishing the situation. "Not the whole weekend."

Nick pulled away from her. "You better tell me what you're up to."

"Nothing happened, Nick. What's the matter? Can't handle the other side of the coin, huh?", giving a sarcastic little laugh.

Her attitude enraged him. Now he was yelling. "Well, so you're cheating on me? You'll regret it."

She yelled right back. "Who do you think you are? You never come home anymore. I didn't cheat on you, but I sure could have if I wanted."

Sleepy-eyed Kimmie walked right in between them and hugged her momma's leg, "Hi Mom."

"Hi, baby!" Liz wrapped her into a tight embrace.

"Will you sleep with me tonight, Momma?"

"Sure, sweetie." Liz carried Kimmie to her room and closed the door behind her. Nick sat in the living room seething and forming a plan to get even.

Over the next few weeks, Nick could not get answers about Liz's "wild weekend." He stayed away more than ever. Most nights, he came home after their little girl was already asleep. Usually, he slept on the couch. He and Liz were not making love anymore, anyway.

Other than a twinge or two over not seeing much of Kimmie, Nick no longer felt guilty about hitting the bars after work. A switch had flipped in his mind; he felt justified to pursue the right of happiness now. He called Sheila from his work phone to plan their evening.

REFLECT…

Are you feeling loss right now? The loss of a relationship or the feeling that the loss is coming soon? Are you worried about how this will affect your children? Maybe you are struggling to keep your relationship afloat or even considering ending it.

> "Make a decision to do your part right now to stop the cycle of inflecting hurts on each other. You will find that there is power and grace in such a choice."

Take some time and think about things alone. Then, look at your child for one long moment. Be silent and still and look at her. She needs your best efforts in this world. I know it's not easy doing the right thing, especially when the idea of a new love feels amazing. The want is irresistible. Just imagine how much better you will feel on the inside knowing you tried everything. I mean really tried.

If you want things to change, you've got to start somewhere. Are you ready to begin?

APPLY…

- Schedule a "date night" with your partner and make it happen frequently.

Never forget you were a couple first.

Your family needs the primary relationship to stay primary.

Parenting is stressful. The modern world is stressful. Getting away from the kids and focusing on each other is critical for you and your family's health and happiness.

- Slow things down on the relationship front.

Relationships happen in cycles, like everything else.

It doesn't matter where you are at this moment. Take a look at the choices you made that led you to this point. Is this your second marriage or primary relationship? What is your cycle?

If your desires are ruling you, your cycle will continue. The want wins every time. A new relationship feels fresh and clean. You get to start over. The resentments and frustrations in the old relationship seem to be absent from this one. It feels like a cure for what is ailing you. Is it a cure or just another peg on a cycle of wants?

- If you have been considering leaving, you might try to strengthen your marriage or relationship by doing some things your partner has been asking you to do.

Doing good with expectation of nothing in return can break negative cycles.

Can you stop the momentum of a breakup? Maybe, if you truly want to do so. Are you willing to stop the cheating/breakup behavior? Even for a week? The Five Percent Rule means making one small change and then building on the momentum it creates.

A program called "iMarriage" can take each partner out of the orbit of his or her self- interest and into putting the relationship on a higher plane.

Is there another way of life besides retaliating? Of course! Make a decision to do your part right now to stop the cycle of inflicting hurts. You will find there is power and grace in such a choice.

Listen to your partner. Find his or her perspective on problems in the relationship. Then, resolve to do something positive on your end. Make some changes, without expectations for a return favor. For example, if your partner is complaining that you are away from home too much, try coming home early from work once a week. The happiness in the home will be elevated and the stress reduced. Small victories birth more small victories.

- Get a neutral professional to help you.

There are excellent relationship therapists. Find one and give it your best shot.

Do you find yourself involved in the same argument with your lover again and again?

The relationship is in a kind of trap. A good counselor can help unspring the trap and get the two of you communicating again. There are talented and caring counselors in the world. They are trained to help couples. Choose one carefully, as therapists are hit and miss on the working chemistry. If the first one does not feel right, try a second one and even a third one.

RESOURCE TOOLBOX

- iMarriage Study Guide, (DVD and book) produced by Northpoint Resources, North Point Ministries, 4400 North Point Parkway, Suite 100, Alpharetta, Georgia 30022. (Northpointministries.org).
- American Association for Marriage and Family Therapy. www.aamft.org.

BABY MAMMAS AND BABY DADDIES:

Too Young to Parent

"For you know that we dealt with each of you as a father deals with his own children, encouraging, comforting and urging you to live lives worthy of God, who calls you into his kingdom and glory." 1 Thessalonians 2:11-12 (NIV)

"I don't want to go, what's the point?"

"You need to at least hear what they have to say, and the DNA test is mandatory, Victor."

"I'm not doing it, Mom. I told ya, Abbi said it wasn't my baby. She isn't even talking to me anymore."

"Well, if you wind up getting in trouble with the courts, you won't be living in this house anymore. Good grief, Victor, you're twenty years old. You're not sixteen." His mother's glance was cutting.

"Fine, I'll go, but it's a bunch of BS."

Just before 10 am the next morning, Victor was roused by his mom's fifth yell. He was scared to go to the prosecutor's office, all he wanted to do was to go back to sleep.

He drove to his friend Tatum's apartment. They smoked marijuana in front of a big-screen TV. It was escape time, and they joked back and forth for a while. Victor sprayed some cologne on his shirt and neck to hide the potent pot odor before heading out.

Victor walked to the courthouse in a stoned, scared daze. He shuffled into the prosecutor's office and stood in front of the receptionist's station awkwardly. Fear was making Victor's mind cloudy; he just wanted it to be over.

"Can I help you, sir?"

He smiled at the pretty office worker. His eyes held hers a moment too long.

"What can I do for you?" Her voice was firm and impatient.

"Oh, I, uh, am supposed to be meeting with a prosecutor lady about a DNA test."

"Are you Victor Krouse?"

"Yeah."

"Well, we will need to see some identification, such as your driver's license."

"Oh, okay." Victor fumbled for his wallet. His fingers did not seem to be working normally; he felt slightly faint.

"Let me get a copy of your license. Go ahead and take a seat, Mr. Krouse."

A few minutes later he was called into a small conference room. Victor was intimidated by the unsmiling woman in a business suit sitting across from him.

"We are requesting that you submit to a paternity test to determine if you are the father of Braydon Renfrow, born March 28, 2014. Are you willing to sign a stipulation to do the testing, or will we need to obtain a court order compelling you to do so?"

"I, uh, don't know what to do."

"Mr. Krouse, have you given any thought what you would like to do in the event this child turns out to be your son?"

"No, uh, I already have a daughter that I'm supposed to be paying a hundred and eighty-eight dollars per month to her mom. I just don't have any money."

The deputy prosecutor looked at him intently. "How old is your other child, and do you visit with her?"

"She's three. Right now her mom is mad at me and not letting me see her."

The prosecutor shook her head at the all too familiar pattern. "Well, are you going to sign this paternity testing stipulation or not?"

Victor signed the forms, promising that he would present himself at a local medical clinic to provide a DNA sample.

His mother made sure he complied by driving him to the appointment.

A month after the DNA test, Victor received papers in the mail. He did not understand their meaning. The papers did not say he was Braydon's father. Instead, they stated Victor was "not excluded as the father of Braydon Renfrow." There was also a number listed, "99.99 %."

Victor's mother knew what the papers meant, and she was angry. "So, you have a second child now, Vic. What are you going to do about it?"

Victor wanted more than anything to get out of there, to head over to Tatum's. His mind was blank. "I don't know, Mom."

"Well, I've had it up to here with your irresponsibility and your pot smoking. I'm giving you one week to find a job and come up with a plan for helping out with this baby boy of yours. You are also going to sign this." She thrust a piece of paper into his hands.

As Victor read the "AGREEMENT," he winced. The second line had him promising to stop using marijuana. He wasn't worried about the $200.00 per month rent; he would come up with it somehow. Victor signed the paper, with a plan already in mind. *I will really have to be careful now about the pot smell when I come home.*

"One more thing, Victor. You and I are going to meet with Abbi and her parents. I can't stand this anymore. Your baby needs a daddy, and you are going to step up to the plate this time around."

Back at Tatum's, the two of them got high, then talked about things. Tatum threw a succession of wild, stoned ideas at Victor. He could get a job on a cruise ship to Europe. He could road trip across the country. He could try to sell his artwork on the streets, or even get a real job.

All the plans sounded reasonable to Victor, but reality kept crashing in. "All I know is my mom's serious about kickin' me out if I don't get a job."

Tatum always had an answer. "Well, smoke another bowl and go to the job service, man."

A week later, Victor got a part-time job at Burger King. His mother was satisfied enough with this sign of progress to not question him about marijuana use.

Abbi Renfrow lived with her parents in a split-level home in the hills overlooking Bayview. Her father was principal of an elementary school nearby. Abbi was a shy eighteen-year-old who looked sixteen. Her parents made her stop seeing Victor. Although she didn't like it, Abbi went along with their demand.

The two grandmothers had set up a meeting between the families. Abbi and her parents sat at their kitchen table, waiting for Victor and his mother to arrive.

"Dad, please don't say anything embarrassing to them."

"What could I say to embarrass this young man? I don't think he is capable of being embarrassed."

They heard a knock.

The five of them sat around the table. Victor's eyes were locked onto the placemat in front of him. Abbi's father felt anger surging inside of him.

Mr. Renfrow took the lead. "So, how do you young folks intend to raise Braydon?"

As if on cue, the baby awoke with a cry. Abbi didn't stir; her mother popped up to check on him. She warmed up a bottle and fed Braydon at the table. Victor's mother ticked his toes, while Victor looked mutely at his son.

"Well?" asked Mr. Renfrow. He looked at Abbi.

"I don't know, Dad. What am I supposed to say?"

"How about you, Victor. Any ideas to share with us?"

"Well, I do have a job now. I would like to have Braydon live with mom and me half the time."

Mrs. Renfrow shook her head disapprovingly. Noticing her husband was about to lay down the law, his wife spoke quickly.

"Braydon is too young. He needs to have one stable home. We certainly have no problem with you coming over here to see him, Victor."

"I should get to have him too. I have rights."

Mr. Renfrow couldn't stop himself. "With rights come responsibilities. So far, you haven't shown any willingness to meet responsibilities. Don't you have another child?"

"Well, yeah, but. . ."

Mr. Renfrow's authoritarian voice silenced Victor. "No buts about it. You and your mother are welcome to come over here and visit Braydon, as long as you are courteous and respectful."

Victor was silent, but his mother was not.

"Mr. Renfrow, you are not calling the shots here. I am not saying my son has done everything correctly. However, as the father of this boy, he does have rights. We are willing to start out slow with visits, but we should be allowed to have those visits at our own home." She looked at Abbi for any hint of support or empathy, but Abbi was too intimidated by her father to meet anyone's eyes.

Mr. Renfrow said, "Victor will need to show us he can be responsible before we even consider that."

The moment's silence was oppressive.

"Come on, Victor, I believe we should go now." Mother and son stood.

Mrs. Renfrow walked with them to the door. Ever the peacemaker, she kept her soothing voice as she called out to them. "You two can call if you want to come see the baby, okay?"

Victor was already walking down the steps, but his mother turned towards Mrs. Renfrow and said angrily, "We are not going to let this go. We will take this to court if we have to."

Mrs. Renfrow's smile vanished as she closed the door quickly.

At his mother's urging, Victor met with a low-income court advocate who helped him file a parenting plan case. The advocate suggested they baby proof their house and create a space for Braydon. A home inspection was scheduled the following month.

Victor felt a surge of pride as he glanced inside the baby room. Nothing was out of place, it looked perfect. The baby crib and bassinet were brand new. One corner was piled high with stuffed animals that looked like they had just been won at a fair. The blue and red wallpaper was covered with speeding race cars and waving flags. No one could look at the baby room without saying, "Adorable."

Victor was the only person who wasn't aware of the cold feel of the room. It was like a dead person's room, tidied and boarded up, only at the reverse stage of life. No baby cries or coos had ever come from within those walls.

The home inspector felt the vacancy inside the showcase room immediately. She made no comment. Victor was disappointed. Ten days later her two-page report came in the mail. The conclusion was matter-of-fact: "I find Mr. Krouse's residence to be adequate for a child."

Victor sat in the court advocate's small, windowless office. They reviewed the paperwork Abbi's lawyer had filed in response to Victor's case. There were pages and pages of accusations. Victor was a "drug addict, a neglectful parent, irresponsible." One document ordered Victor to submit to a hair follicle drug test. Victor's stomach heaved; the room suddenly felt suffocating. He needed to leave.

The advocate handed Victor a blank declaration form. "You will need to respond by filling out this declaration. You can have family members and other people who know you do the same. Unfortunately, my role is to help you with paperwork; you are on your own in court."

Head down, Victor grabbed the papers and walked out.

The next two weeks passed by in a hazy blur. Victor rarely went home. His mother knew what he was doing, but she did not have it in her to throw him out with court looming.

The morning of the temporary order hearing, Victor's mother couldn't reach him on the phone. She left several messages; she even drove to Tatum's apartment. No one answered the door. She drove dispiritedly to court.

She joined a row of tense people sitting on the benches inside courtroom five. Every few seconds she tossed her head back to see if her son had arrived. The room was full of people, including the Renfrows, but no Victor.

When the case was called, a bailiff boomed out, "Victor Krouse." Instead of Victor, his mother stood up. "I am Victor's mother, sir, can I speak?"

The judge looked at her sympathetically. "I am sorry, ma'am, but you cannot. You are not a party to this case."

Abbi's lawyer stood up. "Your Honor, since Mr. Krouse has not seen fit to show up to his own court case, I have orders to present to you. We are requesting that he submit to a hair follicle test and that no visitation be ordered until the results are in. We have serious concerns about Mr. Krouse's fitness to parent."

The judge signed the orders without comment.

Abbi returned home with her parents. She played with Braydon for seven minutes, then left him to her mother's care and hurried to her computer to make a Facebook report to friends about the court hearing.

REFLECT…

It's normal to avoid things that are upsetting to you. No one wants to feel bad. And yet, until you stand up to the big ones, they keep whittling away your happiness and nagging at your gut.

"Think of your life as though it is a series of building blocks. Make your platform stronger. The platform is you!"

Have you ever had the scary thought that something—perhaps something bad—was going to happen in your life and then stopped thinking about it because it was too uncomfortable? Now is the time to feel the discomfort and continue along. Find a quiet place and think about your life for a little while. Don't try to solve anything, and don't be hard on yourself.

APPLY…

- Just for today, spend a little more time with your child.

One day at a time, you will improve your relationship with your child and your parenting skills.

First things, first. Just for today, spend a little more time with your child. You will feel good about yourself, the clean and loving kind of good.

- Slow down on the relationship front.

We live in a "throwaway society," but people are not throwaways!

Hurrying into new relationships while in the middle of child custody drama leads to poor judgment and more relationship failures. Slow down. Think of your life as though it is a series of building blocks. Make your platform stronger. The platform is you! This means facing up to your problems honestly and taking advice about ways to address them. It also means devoting your energy to the people already in your life, especially your child.

If you are a father with limited custodial rights, take steps to build a good relationship with child number one before you start a custody battle against a second "baby mama." Put aside your resentment for a moment. Slow down. If you do not stop traveling around a circle, your life will circle in a downward arc.

- If you are going to help someone financially, then tie benchmarks in with the help.

Tough love is still love! It works, it really does.

Young adults are often unable to afford living on their own. Their parents want to help, while also leading their adult children towards responsibility. It will not happen by cushioning consequences.

A job and/or college is a good beginning benchmark. It is also helpful to put into writing the deal-breakers, the bottom-line behaviors that you just won't tolerate. A written contract can make consequences clear for second unplanned pregnancies and drug use while living at home. There is an old saying that the way to determine if an addict is lying is by whether his mouth is open! Hair follicle drug testing is a great tool to get past the lies told by addicts. A hair follicle test can provide a use history going back several months, and the tests are more difficult to adulterate or alter than urine tests.

RESOURCE TOOLBOX

- Biddulph, Steve, 2002, The Secret of Happy Children: Why Children Behave the Way They Do – and What You Can Do to Help Them Be Loving, Optimistic, Capable and Happy (Marlowe and Company).
- Galinsky, Ellen, 2010, Mind in the Making: The Seven Essential Life Skills Every Child Needs (HarperStudio).

STEP-OUT PARENTING:

Blended Families

"If it is possible, as far as it depends on you, live at peace with everyone." Romans 12:18 (NIV)

"Just go away, go on, get out!" Sheryl yelled. Her step-dad Lonnie walked out of the room, but not before firing back an angry reply.

"Don't ask me for anything, Sheryl, if you are going to treat me like that." She buried her face in her pillow, full of hate.

Lonnie closed Sheryl's door and climbed back into bed beside Tara. "It doesn't matter what I do, Tara. I could be a saint for ten years and it wouldn't make any difference."

Tara started to repeat the tired words "things will get better," but then she saw how hopelessly defeated he was. *Wow, a new low. I didn't think things could get any worse*. Her spirits sank with his. There was nothing to say that could fix it.

"I have to go to sleep; I can't talk now." She turned the light off and scooted to the edge of the bed away from him.

Lonnie and Tara had kept their relationship hidden from their second graders for almost two months. After that, they couldn't keep their promise to each other to "take things slowly." Time to be together.

Tara brought Happy Meals, snacks and enthusiasm to the park for the first meeting. She smiled at Sheryl as they parked and stepped into the sunlight. Lonnie and his daughter, Mindie, were watching them nervously.

Each girl hung close to her parent as Tara made introductions. They said “hi” to each other and sat down at a picnic table awkwardly. Tara tried to jump start conversation for the girls, but each time it ended in strained silence.

“Why don’t you two go play at the playground?”

“I don’t want to, Mom.” Both girls sat frozen at the table.

“You two go play, now.” Lonnie said forcefully.

Mindie and Sheryl walked sullenly toward the play castle. Mindie climbed the monkey bars as Sheryl sat on a teeter-totter looking in the opposite direction.

After they ate, Tara and Lonnie walked away from the girls to debrief.

“That went well, don’t you think?” Tara forcing a weak laugh.

“This is all new to them; it will take time.” Lonnie tried to sound confident, but he felt a flicker of doubt inside as he picked up their trash.

A week later, Lonnie and Mindie were sitting in their condo talking.

“We are going to have pizza with Tara and Sheryl, what do you think about that?”

“I would rather just go with you, Dad.”

“Well, hon, you need to understand that Tara and I are a couple. We love each other. In fact, the four of us are going to be living together as soon as we find a house to rent.”

Mindie looked at her father with a start. As she started to complain, her father cut her off.

“We are going to make this work, Mindie. You’ll see. It will be like having a sister.”

After that, things changed for the girls with warp speed.

The four of them met at the mall and ate lunch in the food court. Lonnie took the lead.

“We have a surprise to show you, after this.”

“What is it, Dad?” asked Mindie.

“You’ll just have to wait and see.” He winked at Tara.

They climbed into Lonnie's Jeep Grand Cherokee and drove across town. Lonnie pulled into the driveway of an older, but well-maintained house.

Tara walked ahead. "Come on girls, look at the room you're gonna share."

Sheryl and Mindie walked into their new bedroom wordlessly. A bunk-bed, complete with ladder and stuffed animals, was against the wall of the small room.

Tara pointed in the direction of a television set on the far wall. "Look, there's a PlayStation set up in here. We got you some games, too."

Sheryl put a game in and sat down to play. Mindie sat on the bottom bunk looking around.

Ten days later they moved into their new home.

Mindie would have adjusted fine to things; unfortunately, she knew Sheryl hated her guts. So Mindie avoided her by watching TV when she was home. She slept on the living room couch. Lonnie carried her back to her bedroom a few times, but Mindie would always make her way back to the couch during the night.

A few weeks after moving into the home, Lonnie was driving Mindie home from her dance class. She dropped a bombshell on her dad.

"Dad, can I live with Mom, mostly? I'd still visit you on the weekends."

Lonnie was stung. He paused for a second. "Why, hon? Don't you think our schedule with your mom has been working out okay?"

"I just want to live with Mom."

"Does it have anything to do with moving in with Tara and Sheryl? I know you and Sheryl are having to adjust to things."

"I hate them."

Shocked that Tara was on the hate list too, Lonnie spoke fast. "You can't mean that, Mindie. I know things have been hard, but Tara's been awfully nice to you; I'm surprised to hear you say that."

"You don't even know, Dad. They're mean, especially Sheryl."

Lonnie's tone grew frustrated. "What has she done that's mean?"

"I don't know, Dad. She just is."

Lonnie had heard enough. "Well, we are not changing our parenting schedule, so you need to get used to the way things are around here. We will all try to do better, okay?"

Mindie nodded, but neither of them felt reassured.

A few days later, Lonnie came home from work to a buzz of activity and trouble. He could hear Tara talking loudly with Sheryl in the girls' bedroom. He poked his head inside. Mindie wasn't in the room. She wasn't anywhere inside. Looking outside, Lonnie spotted her next to a bush along a corner of the house. She was crying.

"What's the matter, honey?"

"I didn't take Sheryl's stupid comb and brush set. They keep saying I did. They are lying!" All her bad feelings poured forth into hysterical sobs.

Lonnie pulled her into his arms. "Okay, take it easy. I will go talk to them. I'll be right back okay?"

He walked into the girls' room. Tara was looking through dresser drawers as Sheryl sat scowling on the bottom bunk bed.

Tara was angry. "You need to talk to your daughter, Lonnie. That brush set she took was a gift from her father. It means a lot to her."

"Well, how do you know she took it? It could have been misplaced."

"We've looked all over. Sheryl keeps it in her top drawer, and now it's gone."

Lonnie's stomach felt twisted. He took a deep breath and fought off the desire to curse at the two of them. He motioned to Tara for them to talk alone. She followed him into their bedroom.

Lonnie unloaded his pent-up frustration on her. "I really resent Mindie being accused of stealing this brush or whatever it is. It was probably misplaced. Your daughter treats her terribly. You two are making her life feel cold here, and I am sick of it."

"Don't play that game with me, Lon. Your daughter is just as much to blame as mine for the two of them not getting along."

Lonnie resisted the urge to yell at her. They stood staring at each other. A wall had materialized between them quite suddenly. The room was wracked with tension. He broke the silence first. "I am taking Mindie away for a few days. I can't go on like this."

"Fine, run away with her. That'll solve everything."

Lonnie ignored her as he walked outside. "Mindie, get your stuff together. We are going to spend a couple days together, just you and me."

Mindie stayed quiet on the outside, but she was overjoyed. It was the best words she had heard in quite a while. She motored into her room and stuffed some clothes into the gym bag she used between her mother's and father's homes.

Lonnie mouthed a sad goodbye to Tara as he walked out the front door.

They drove for an hour to a nice motel with a pool and hot tub. Mindie felt like she had won a victory of some kind. Yet, her mood darkened from time to time as she thought about having to go home to Tara and Sheryl.

The next morning, Lonnie stepped outside to call Tara. They were both happy to hear the other's voice.

"I'm sorry for overreacting."

"So am I. When are you coming home?"

"I promised Mindie two days, so we will be home tomorrow afternoon. What can we do to make things better?"

"Maybe you two needed a few days away. Maybe we all need a getaway. School will be out in three weeks. Let's all go somewhere. By the way, we owe your daughter an apology. Sheryl's brush set turned up in her room."

On their return drive, Mindie had a question.

"Dad, do I still have to live with them, because I don't want to."

"Yes, we are going to make this work, Mindie. While you are with your mother, I want you to think about how you can do your part to help us all get along, okay?"

"Okay, Dad, but I want it to be just you and me."

Lonnie shook his head in frustration. "As usual, there is nothing I can do or say; it's just impossible." He felt like turning the car around and driving far away. Instead, he dropped off Mindie at her mother's with a big hug.

Four days later, Lonnie and Tara called a family conference. The girls walked stiffly to the living room couch and sat at opposite ends.

Tara took the lead. "You two might as well get used to the fact the four of us are going to be living together. We are a family. You two will be a lot happier if you manage to get along. Don't you think so?" She looked at both girls as she waited for a reply. No one spoke.

"All right, we will start with you, Sheryl. Why don't you make an effort to be friends with Mindie?"

"I don't know, Mom."

"You can do better than that. We can stay here until you decide to participate."

"She just annoys me, that's all. She takes my stuff. I need my own room" Mindie gave her a cutting look.

"You know that's not possible right now. So, what about you, Mindie? Any suggestions?"

"I don't know," Mindie said nervously.

Lonnie spoke for the first time. Irritation streamed through his voice. "I've had it with the 'I don't knows.' Nothing is going to get better unless the two of you make an effort to communicate."

Mindie's voice caught in her throat. She wanted to say some things, a lot of things, but she just couldn't. She looked down.

Tara sighed. "Since you two don't want to contribute anything positive, you can both sit in your room all afternoon until you have some ideas to share."

Heads tilted down, the girls walked separately down the hall.

The family conference didn't seem to change anything. Lonnie and Tara put their hope into a vacation. Over the next week, Tara made the arrangements for the trip to Disneyland. She was excited for Sheryl to come home from school.

"Sit down with me a minute, Sheryl. I've got some really great news. The four of us get to go to Disneyland after school is out. We are going to have a great time!"

"Nice, Mom." Sheryl said.

"Don't you want to go to Disneyland?"

"Yeah, sure."

Tara walked away. Even Disneyland didn't melt the ice in this blender of a family. Her thoughts turned bitter. "What's the point in spending money on a trip like that for such ungrateful kids?"

They headed down I-5 towards southern California and Disneyland. Sheryl and Mindie buried their eyes into their iPods and tablets; they hardly spoke to one another.

There was a moment, actually a whole evening, where things felt smooth, even warm. They all felt it. Mindie and Sheryl had ridden a few scary rides together. In the excitement, their mutual dislike was forgotten. That evening, sitting at the Rainforest Café, they talked of their favorite thrills.

"Can we go back tonight?" they both asked.

"No, but we still have tomorrow, girls."

The parents went to sleep happy that night.

REFLECT…

Did the story spark some feelings in you, perhaps some hurt? Are you spending nights worrying about your child's feelings? Maybe your "blended family" isn't

"Imagine how good you will feel if the air is cleared and you and your significant other make progress in accepting things as they are, including everyone's feelings."

blending well, and your dreams feel smashed. The pain and worry are there because you love your family. You want things to work so badly.

While you cannot "fix" things, you have a chance right now to improve things. Please do not be hard on yourself. Imagine how good you will feel if the air is cleared and you and your significant other make progress in accepting things as they are, including everyone's feelings.

APPLY...

- Take an inventory with so much honesty it hurts.

Get a pencil and paper and write down the highs and lows of your life right now.

Record what is working well in your life and what is not working. Then find a trustworthy, caring, and wise person to discuss things.

- Let go off expectations for a perfect family.

Expectations lead to resentments and these explode into conflict.

When your expectations are not met, bitterness and anger are the result. Then comes hurtful words and poor decisions. Letting go of expectations does not mean letting go of hope. It means accepting things as they are and working on things from there.

- Do not push your child to like the new people you brought into his or her life.

Even if you cannot stand what your child says, do not stifle his or her voice.

Allow your child his or her own feelings. A period of adjustment is typical, and it may take longer than you would like. Putting pressure on people to be buddies usually has the opposite effect. Accept the true situation and move forward in truth.

- Spend "one on one" time with your child.

He or she needs to feel special and secure in the midst of big change.

After all, your child has lost the mother and father family unit. Add to that trauma the further sense of loss that comes from having to share a parent with new people.

- Take things slowly in your relationships.

Slowing things down gives you a great opportunity to learn about your new love's character.

Over time, you will see it pay big dividends in your life. How your new love reacts to your child-centered priority will speak volumes about his or her character and the future of your relationship. Yes, it is hard to do when you're in love. It goes against your emotions, especially the need for that perfect relationship.

- Communicate with your child's other parent.

If the other parent is still in the picture, communication can help lower conflict and provide you with information.

Of course, in some cases communication is always full of conflict. Consider sending text messages with short and polite updates about your child. Less emotion is carried through text messaging than voice calls.

- Set a clear boundary about your new love's role in disciplining your child.

Do not allow the stepparent to spank or ever get physical with your child.

The issue of stepparent discipline should be addressed early. Your first duty is to protect and nurture your child. You and the child's other parent (if involved) should be doing the discipline. Yet, if your new partner is going to be providing some care for your child, he or she will have to enforce some rules. Set boundaries on discipline and stick to them.

RESOURCE TOOLBOX

- Stepfamily Foundation Inc. (stepfamily.org).
- Baksh, Nadir and Murphy, Laurie E., 2010, 8 Strategies for Successful Step-Parenting. (Murphy, Hohm Press).

JAIL HOUSE DAD:

Seven Kids with Seven Women

"In everything set them an example by doing what is good. In your teaching show integrity, seriousness." Titus 2:7 (NIV)

"I love my kids."

Ivan Bledsoe sat on the wrong side of a glass partition in the county jail. He was trying to read his lawyer's face through a thick plate-glass window. He didn't trust the man in the suit. "Well, what have you got for me? You gonna get these charges dismissed or what?"

Attorney Evan Pittman paused for effect. Then he spoke deliberately. "Methamphetamine was found in your vehicle, Mr. Bledsoe. That's constructive possession. You will need a witness to convince a jury that the drugs were not yours and that you did not knowingly have them in your vehicle."

"I told you the bag wasn't mine. I just gave a guy a ride. Frank something. I think he lives on Stevenson Avenue."

"How am I supposed to find this Frank on Stevenson Avenue?"

"I don't know." Ivan banged his head on the glass.

"Take a breath, Ivan. I will do my best. You need to be aware this would be your fourth felony. If you go down for it, you're likely to do four years." The lawyer shuffled his papers as if to leave.

"Hold on. I got another thing to talk to ya about. My ex won't let me see my baby boy. Can't you file an emergency motion or something?"

"There's a lot more to it then filing a motion. You would need to start a parentage action in court, serve the child's mother, then bring a motion for visitation. If you are serious about it, my office would need a twenty-five hundred dollar retainer."

Anger fired through Ivan as he thought about Amber keeping his son from him. He stood up. "I'll get you the money. Amber's not gonna pull this on me. Do it."

"I have to ask you some questions. Do you have any other children? If so, what do the court orders say about custody and visitation?"

"Yeah, I've got a daughter, Makenna, in town. I see her sometimes. There's no court order or anything. I've got three other kids that live in Indiana, but I'm not allowed to have any contact with them."

"Why not?"

"CPS has custody of 'em."

"Did Child Protection Services terminate your parental rights?"

"Yeah. I was in prison and couldn't do anything about it. I love my kids."

Mr. Pittman kept his professional cool and didn't reveal his thoughts to Ivan. *Yeah, you sure do. That's why you're in here, instead of being a father to them.*

The lawyer pushed his notepad into a briefcase and snapped it shut. The meeting was over

"Very well, Mr. Bledsoe, get me my retainer and I will begin work on your custody case." Mr. Pittman opened the door to the rear and stepped out.

Back in his cell, Ivan thought about his latest arrest. The weeks leading up to jail were a blur in his mind, like a bad movie played at fast forward. Things started with creaming at Amber. Taking off with a friend and wrecking a car in Ohio. Stealing another car to get home and losing the friend somewhere, with no idea how that went down down. Most of all, being loaded—always loaded and scrounging for money. Then came jail and uncared-for misery; his skin had crawled. Vomiting until the dry heaves came. The jailers had ignored his pleas for pain medication. He was told to bring it up with the jailhouse doctor next week. After the first few days, he had slept twenty hours a day.

Ivan thought about his baby son, Aaron. *"Did I play with him much?"* He knew the answer, and it stung him a little.

His reverie was broken by shouting. Ivan's cellmate, a nineteen-year-old hyperactive drug addict, was jumping up and down on the metal toilet against the back wall, laughing and yelling.

The cellmate got in Ivan's face. "What's with you, man, you're trippin' out."

Ivan thought he had an audience. "Yeah, I was just thinking about my ex and how she won't let me see my kid. There's something wrong with her. She shouldn't even be talking about me. She's always dropping off my kid with people she barely knows."

The cellie ignored him.

From the corridor, a jailer's booming voice interrupted them. "Ivan Bledsoe, come out here; you're wanted in video court."

Family Court Judge Omar Perez was sitting on the bench in his courtroom, watching Ivan come into view on a large television screen.

"You are Ivan Bledsoe?"

"Yes, yes sir."

"The state is represented by Deputy Prosecutor Annie Coupe. Mr. Bledsoe, you previously admitted to being in contempt of court for not paying child support in the amount of two hundred and fourteen dollars per month as ordered. You also waived the right to have an attorney on this case."

"Ms. Coupe, how do you wish to proceed?"

"We are asking for a five-day sanction in jail to run concurrent with the time he is now serving on new criminal matters. We also would like to have Mr. Bledsoe make a payment of at least two hundred dollars within thirty days of release to purge his contempt. He is already over five thousand behind in child support, and our records show he has not made a payment in two years. Perhaps Mr. Bledsoe can enlighten us as to what he intends to do."

Judge Perez watched Ivan's face turn ugly with anger. Ivan was bobbing up and down on his chair.

"Mr. Bledsoe."

Ivan continued to fidget without speaking.

"Mr. Bledsoe! Do you have anything to say?"

"I was in jail, Judge! I can't pay when I'm locked up. Besides, I have other kids, including a baby boy that I've been helping out with."

"Are you ordered to pay support for any other children, Mr. Bledsoe?" Judge Perez asked patiently.

"Yes, for two of them. And like I said, I've been giving diapers to my baby's mom."

"How many children do you have, Mr. Bledsoe?"

"Five, I think."

Judge Perez tried to hide his disgust. *A contempt case for a guy like this. What a waste of our time and energy. I know what I would do if I had the power to do it.* He shook the thought out of his head and refocused on the hearing.

"I will follow the State's requests. Mr. Bledsoe, if you don't get on track with your child support, you will find yourself back in court. The State may not be so lenient with their jail time request next time."

Ivan walked angrily back to his cell. He looked at his cellmate, who was still bouncing off the walls.

"I don't care what they say. She don't let me see the kid, I ain't payin'. I'll just sign my rights away." Ivan cursed at the world.

The cellie continued to flit around the room, ignoring Ivan.

REFLECT…

Are YOU dating someone like that? Does he have two "baby mamas" already? Is he spending time consistently with his child or children? One more question: Is there anything more important about a person than how he or she treats children?

"If you want to predict a person's future actions, the best place to start is with his or her past behavior. A person who neglects his own child is not relationship material."

Perhaps other people are being judgmental towards you. Please don't be hard on yourself. Remember you are a good person who loves your child more than anything. Take some time and think about the past few years. What has gone well and what has gone badly? Now is the time to use the new awareness you have gained to make your child's life and your next child's life much better.

APPLY…

- Talk to an older person whom you trust.

No one has a monopoly on how to live. We all need wise counsel.

If there is no such person, you will need to find one. Discuss your situation. Is the absence of a father hurting your child? What about your next child?

- Slow down on the relationship/sex front.

You cannot go backwards to undo mistakes.

Right now you are going forward, either to new happiness or new problems.

If you want to predict a person's future actions, the best place to start is with his or her past behavior. A person who neglects his own child is not relationship material. Run, don't walk, from someone who feels compelled to explain (i.e. excuse) that past, or pretends it is unimportant. Remember, if you have a child with a "father" who is not really being a father, you cannot make him change. You will not be able to change the next boyfriend either!

- Put some time into developing your talents and growing as a person.

Your growth will insulate you from the next drug-fueled wild child who wants to get close to you!

There will never be a shortage of males willing to make babies without caring for them. The trick is to avoid having another baby with someone else who will not be a loving parent to your child. Young male criminals can sure look like cool rebels. They talk the talk, and they talk fast. And they can furnish drugs on demand. If you develop some self-confidence, you won't want anything to do with men (boys) like this.

RESOURCE TOOLBOX

- Rossi, Kelly A., 2014, Dating the Wrong Men: The Mis-adventurer's Guide Through Bad Relationship Choices. (Social Magnitude, LLC.).

ROCKS OF STABILITY:

Grandparents Raising Their Kid's Kids

"Children are a heritage from the Lord, offspring a reward from him." Psalm 127:3 (NIV)

Doreen and Larry McGarvey were awakened from their nap by the ringing of their landline telephone. Doreen heard a serious sounding voice on the line.

"Mrs. McGarvey, this is Marybeth Rubio. I am a social worker at the Office of Children and Family Services, Child Protective Services.

Doreen stiffened. *Something has happened to Kami or Jonah.*

"Ma'am, you and your husband have been identified as a possible placement for your grandchildren. I am sorry to tell you that your son Rollie and his girlfriend were arrested last night. Their children have been taken into protective custody. Is there any chance you could come to my office today? I can give you more information, and we can talk about sending the children home with you, at least on a temporary basis. Our office is in downtown Buffalo."

Doreen didn't hesitate. "Of course. Larry and I will head right over there."

Forty-five minutes later, they pulled their Buick into a crowded parking lot and headed into the social services office. A stern-faced secretary led them to a conference room. Inside, two social workers sat reviewing papers in manila folders.

One of the social workers stood up. "You must be the McGarveys. Hi, I'm Marybeth Rubio. I have been assigned to your grandchildren's case. This is my supervisor, Kathy Imel."

Doreen nodded. Her voice cracking, she asked: "Where are the kids?"

"You'll see them in just a bit. We need to discuss a temporary placement for them first."

"Of course, we will take them home with us. They've spent a good part of their lives with us. What's Rollie and Lily pulled this time?"

"All I know is they were arrested at their apartment. Apparently, the police found methamphetamine inside the residence. The place was a mess. No food in the house. Your grandchildren were home, and the police called us. We took the children into protective custody. We have already done a criminal background check on the two of you. You can take the children home with you today."

Larry ran his hand across the marble counter. He fixed a curious look at the social workers. "You know, we hadn't planned on raising kids at our age." He managed a slight chuckle.

Doreen looked at him sharply, then turned her gaze to the social workers.

"We love these kids more than anything. They've spent a lot of time with us. Larry may miss a game or two of golf, but he plays too much anyway."

An hour and many forms later, they walked into a playroom. Little Jonah sprang into his grandfather's arms and held on tight. Eight-year-old Kami sat on the floor, sad-eyed and listless. Doreen sat down next to her.

Marybeth Rubio smiled at them. "You all head home and enjoy each other today. Please let me know tomorrow how things are going, Mrs. McGarvey. I will be in touch in the next few days."

As they climbed into the Buick, Jonah started sobbing. "Where are we going, Grandma?"

Doreen leaned in and cradled his head. "You two are coming home with us, hon."

She looked at Larry. "I'm riding in the back with the kids". She sat in the middle and hugged both of them.

Two days later, their son called collect from jail. *Oh no, another one of Rollie's frantic calls. What is he going to manipulate us about this time?*

"You don't understand, Mom. I'm being railroaded by the courts. If you don't hire me a good lawyer, I'm going to prison. Lily took off with some other guy. Last week she threatened to take the kids and run. I don't even know what's gonna happen!"

Rollie rambled in confusing detail about his latest arrest. Doreen pressed her hand against her face. Her head ached. For a second, she considered hanging up on her son. Instead, she sat down at the kitchen table and held the phone a few inches away.

Finally he paused, and she got a word in. "What is it you're asking us to do?"

"I need five thousand to hire a lawyer or I'm toast."

"I will talk to your father and we will make a decision."

This time was different. Larry was as adamant as she was. No more money. No more help that didn't help.

Rollie called again the next day. Doreen clenched her left hand into a fist and tried to steel herself. Her voice cracking, she told him there would be no money this time. She heard cussing, then a click.

The end of the money tree was a long time coming. They paid a lawyer once and a bail bondsman twice. Rollie or Lily would show up to drop Kami and Jonah off at the grandparents with a story about the latest misfortune. The kids would be dirty, tired, and upset. Doreen would shepherd them into the house and glare at whichever parent had come this time. Days would turn into weeks without hearing from Rollie or Lily. Once, Rollie and Lily disappeared for over two months and never once called to speak to their children.

We never should have sent Kami and Jonah back with them that last time. Through all the chaos, Doreen carried a nagging feeling with her. They'd made a lot of mistakes trying to help Rollie. Always bailing him out, especially after the grandchildren were born. She had worried about them constantly.

Kami had been the one to let things slip out. They were moving again.

"Mom is always sick in bed. The police came over last night." A teary blurting out, "They took Daddy to jail, Grandma!"

Doreen put her hands on her knees. Rollie's troubles were his alone now. The children's hurt was her hurt. At least it was clear what they had to do.

Weeks passed. She was amazed by the kids' resilience. How quickly they adjusted to major change! Jonah, especially, was carefree and happy in their home. He lit up like a firefly when Grandpa paid attention to him. Even Kami was coming around. She liked helping Doreen cook.

One evening, the four of them sat on the living room couch watching reruns of "Full House." Doreen had been shocked by the TV shows Kami wanted to watch and by the amount of time she spent in front of the TV. She was exhausted, fighting the urge to fall asleep.

"Kami, hon, maybe we could invite one of your friends over from your old neighborhood. How would that be?"

"That'd be okay. I wish Missy could come over, but I don't have her phone number."

"Well, I'll get Grandpa to take us over there and see about getting you two girls together. Maybe tomorrow."

Doreen saw Kami's face brighten. She hugged her.

The next morning Doreen went outside to talk to Larry in his shop. Jonah was stomping on a piece of wood and sweating with the effort. That boy loves working with wood!

She put her hand on Larry's shoulder. "We've got to keep things as normal as possible for these kids. We are going to drive into Buffalo this morning and try to find one of Kami's friends. I'm also worried about school in September. I have no idea how long they will be with us, and neither does the social worker. They probably can't go to their old school. It's an hour away."

Larry grunted a quick "okay" and turned back to his workbench to watch Jonah. An hour later, Larry moaned and groaned as he drove the four of them into the city.

REFLECT…

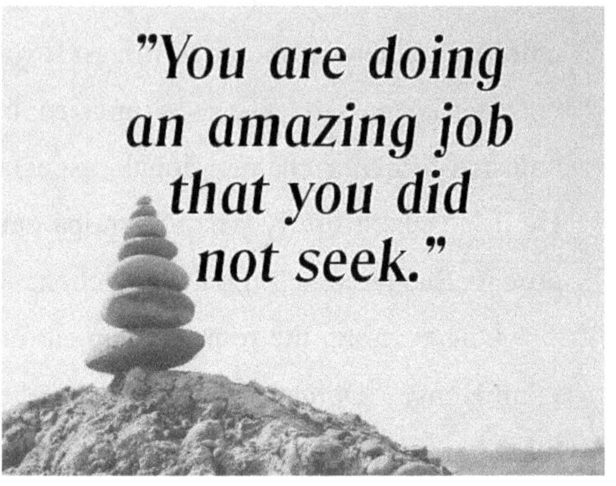

Did this story touch your heart? It hurts so much to feel the pain of a family torn apart. How hard it must be to perform the role of parent and grandparent at the same time. Despite the exhaustion and hurt, you continue loving on the kids. It's just what you do.

Maybe God has people living longer than they did fifty years ago because He knew of the mess society would make of parenting. You are doing an amazing job that you did not seek.

Life feels cruel and hopeless sometimes. You probably need more help. So many grandparents do. Help is out there. Maybe you also need a sense that things are going to be okay in the long run. Please continue reading for some suggestions to help you and the kids.

APPLY…

- Ask for help!

You need help. Go out and get some.

Please do not carry the burden alone. Perhaps you are the kind of person who grew up believing one must "tough it out" instead of talking about pain and loss. You cannot be effective in caring for children in crisis all by yourself. Reach out to people. Tell your friends and neighbors a little bit about your situation. You don't need to disclose all the messy details. Just let them know you need help. Even a short break a few times a week will allow you needed rest.

Talk to the social workers about your needs. See if respite care is available. If you have a church, meet with the pastor or a trusted member and tell him or her what is going on in your life. Find a good therapist to help untwist the painful knots of a situation gone wrong.

- Dealing with Child Protective Services is difficult and complicated. Get advice from a good attorney.

Social workers are like everyone else. Yours may be a gem or a disaster.

If you are having problems with Child Protection Services or even if you have unanswered questions, sit down with a lawyer experienced in those cases. The consultation fee will be well worth the money.

Child Protective Services performs unpleasant and stressful tasks. Many of these agencies are overburdened. Dealing with C.P.S. can be difficult and frustrating. The system involves difficult choices and, often, unhappy endings. Anyone involved with the agency should properly arm themselves with information about the procedures and rights involved in the case.

Find out what the child protection workers and the judge expect from you and from the biological parents of the children. Learn about the system. You have rights, too. Some Child Protective Services have an "ombudsman" or an advocate for persons with a C.P.S. case. Take the time to meet with such persons. The knowledge you gain will be invaluable. Even if you learn that your social worker is doing an admirable job, this is still very good information as you move forward in the case.

- Get yourself some help to stop enabling the addict in your life.

If you suspect you are enabling someone else, you probably are.

Instead of gratitude, many grandparents receive attacks and blame from their own children. Addicts can be vicious when confronted with the truth about their sad situation.

Enabling a drug addict traps you in the addict's vicious cycles. The "help" that enablers provide actually does more harm than good. Your Child Protection social worker will be watching you closely to determine whether you can protect children from neglectful or abusive parents. Enabling behaviors will impact your chances of persuading C.P.S. and a court that grandchildren should be placed in your care.

Try to establish clear boundaries with your adult sons and daughters. Those boundaries will help you to protect the children and to distance yourself from the blame game the biological parents may try to play. Ask your social worker if there is a support group available for you.

Another good place to gain strength and learn how to set boundaries is Al-Anon, a support group and more for people affected by someone else's substance abuse. These meetings can be found in every state.

RESOURCE TOOLBOX

- American Association of Retired Persons (AARP). See "Guide for GrandFamilies." (AARP.org).
- Brown, Deborah E. and Toledo, Sylvie, 2013, Grandparents as Parents: A Survival Guide for Raising a Second Family. (Guilford Publications).

A CALL FOR NEW HOPE AND FAITH

We do not have a ton of choices in this world. We really have two choices. One is to keep doing the same things again and again, while we avoid facing the things that hurt us and others. The second is to look right in the eye of the problem, with honesty and a little bravery.

Our modern world offers so many pathways along with glittery distractions. Many of the trails lead to destruction. I see many people walking these paths, although they do not believe this is so. Things look glittery, fun and easy until the traps are sprung. And when they are sprung, people cannot see up for down, let alone find a way out.

To change, we will need help from outside of our own trapped mind. Help is out there if you seek it. This means admitting our weaknesses and mistakes. It means putting aside intellectual biases and hardheartedness. And it means exploring faith and spirituality. Isn't it surprising how being humble is actually a sign of strength?

I understand how hard it is to change; I struggle to change my ways. I must remember that it is actions that really show the love in the heart. Mumbled apologies in the midst of pain won't do. If you wish to help your children, be honest with yourself about your problems and take action today to make a change.

INTRODUCTION TO PART III: SELF-DESTRUCTORS: DRUGS AND ALCOHOL

It is no secret that substance abuse is destroying American families. The pain of loving an addict is unbearable and can go on for years and years. Life may not make much sense. But there is hope. As a companion to this epidemic, new treatment and recovery programs continue to emerge. Many substance abusers are now in recovery.

In 2017, there were 70,237 drug overdose deaths. This number increased by 9.6% from 2016. Opiates were responsible for over two-thirds of these deaths. Behind every one of these unfortunate deaths is a tragic story involving a family.

Anxiety is also rampant today. People suffering from anxiety and stress need relief. The worse the pain, the more relief needed. One of the tragedies of our times is that this equation has fostered a resurgence of heroin use, and widespread abuse of powerful narcotic prescription medications, including fentanyl.

Of course, substances merely delay pain, which comes back stronger each time.

Drugs that are dispensed in a friendly medical office may seem safe and clean. If you are looking forward to getting hold of narcotic pain medicine, you are on the road to a serious problem.

Alcoholism and drug addiction are both rides on a sinking ship. However, the powerful drugs many young people use today lead to a fast descent towards destruction. Some alcoholics manage to hold onto jobs and even families for a long time. Things worsen gradually. However, there are no "functioning meth addicts".

Non-addicts are amazed to watch someone in recovery, with everything to lose by using drugs again, relapse. It really is not so surprising. An addict is one bad thought and a quick action away from getting high again.

When the addict crashes, everything becomes transparent and understood. The crash makes everything clear to everyone, even to the addict herself—but only for a moment. Sadly, self-delusion often returns.

Fear of consequences only hangs around for so long. Time makes fear recede into the background, making it easy for an addict's brain to grasp the trick that, "It'll be different this time" or, "I won't overdo it, I just need to take the edge off today." For an addict, it is never 'different this time.' The vicious cycle repeats itself in a downward slope.

Being locked up or placed on probation may create enforced sobriety for a while. However, unless a person is **internally motivated** to remain sober, it will not last.

The truth is that recovery is elusive and mysterious. One addict gets sober and wants to stay that way. Another cannot do so, no matter how much her loved ones wish it. Sorrows and misfortunes abound. The downhill slide seems to go on forever.

Amidst such pain, I ask that you please be open to spiritual solutions. Most experts will admit that they hold no foolproof way to create internal motivation.

Remember: *Conflict* causes
Consequences that require
Help, which brings
Hope that leads to
Resolution.

The stories in this section all touch on substance use, including alcohol. One story looks at the origins of seeking relief with chemicals, through the eyes of our children. They watch as we open containers to feel good and change our mood. What message are you sending?

Whether you are an alcoholic/addict or a loved one, you will find some answers to consider at the end of each story. I know so many of you are hurting. Take a moment and imagine how good you will feel on the inside once you make a beginning. Use the Five Percent Rule to make a small change today. Nothing more is required besides willingness and a starting point.

There are other kinds of relief in the universe besides narcotics!

FUNCTIONAL:

Dad's Growing Alcoholic Monster

"Woe to those who rise early in the morning to run after their drinks, who stay up late at night till they are inflamed with wine."
Isaiah 5:11(NIV)

Alex had started noticing the itch, the one in his brain. A nervous, slightly irritable itch, materializing with the coming of afternoon. It meant one thing: he needed a drink.

"Beer thirty," that mysterious time of day when a drink was well-earned and, for some individuals, a necessity, seemed to be arriving earlier. He didn't worry about it too much. *It's just the stress of this job. They're always wanting more out of us.*

Alex would stop at Bucky's Tavern after work for a couple of beers. Usually, a couple of co-workers joined him. A few drinks transformed him from a tired and money-stressed HVAC repairman to one of the coolest regular guys around.

The couple of beers was actually more like six or seven. After a few late nights, Alex had promised his wife he would be home by 6:00 p.m. each night. Most of the time, he managed to do it.

Lucia commented frequently on his drinking. She lectured, yelled, withheld sex, and negotiated. Often, she suggested he only drink on weekends.

"You don't understand the pressure I'm under at work. And we're barely paying the bills. If it's not one thing, it's another. A few beers after work isn't too much to ask for."

She fumed if he was two minutes late on his promised time. Their arguments grew more heated, yet the words were always the same.

"You just don't care about us! All you care about is drinking with your friends. How would you like it if I started going out drinking all the time?"

"Get off my back. I work myself exhausted for you and the kids, and all I get is complaints."

Sometimes, they made up, with tired promises to "try harder" or "do better." More and more often, they ended up sleeping apart. Bitterness had lodged into each of their hearts, like moisture slowly rotting the underside of a board.

Sitting in his work truck, Alex waited for the light to change. To the right, tucked into a small space between a laundromat and a deli, he spied a wooden sign reading "Bar." That was all. No neon here, yet his eyes were transfixed. *I've got twenty minutes before my next service call.*

Stuck in the left lane, he edged the pickup into traffic to the right. A horn blared at him as he cut off a car and swung into the parking lot.

Pushing back the rising sense of wrongdoing within him, Alex stepped into the bar. It had seen better days. Two empty tables were underneath single-bulb overhead lights. One of them was burned out. Several of the barstool cushions were ripped. He glanced at the one other customer, a thin elderly man with a splotchy red face. Alex ordered a beer and downed a third in one quick swallow.

Instantly, his nerves steadied and brain quieted. The world was looking up. Alex glanced around the place, transformed. He saw a comfortable, inviting bar. He finished the drink and ordered another.

"Here she goes!" He nodded amiably at the bartender and took a big slug of the foamy draft. That one went fast too. He saw the bartender watching him, with a bored expression on his face. "Alright, give me one more. Then I gotta run."

Still seated at the bar, he texted his office that he was stuck in traffic and would be a little late for the service call. As he walked outside, he pulled out the Lifesavers he always kept in his pocket, stuffing a few in his mouth.

He noticed the sunshine and stopped for a moment before leaving. *Wow! I haven't felt this good for a long time. I'm even being careful and not overdoing things.* He fired up the pickup and gunned it as he entered traffic, sending out a plume of black smoke.

The day rolled along smoothly after that. It was almost six o'clock when he dropped off the service vehicle. Before going home, he stopped at his favorite watering hole. *I'll leave after two beers.* He knew it wasn't going to work for his wife, but there was no way he was going home without having a few drinks first.

Cocooned with a heavy buzz, Alex made it home about 8:30 p.m. He slipped on the hallway rug, caught himself from falling and laughed. His wife stood at the end of the hall, glaring at him.

"Oh, you decided to come home, did you?"

"Of course. I always come home for my sweetie." Arms outstretched, Alex hurried to her for a hug.

"Leave me alone." She turned and headed towards the rear of the house.

"Hi, Daddy!" Little Makenzye threw her arms around his ankles, intercepting him as he tried to follow his wife. He played with her and her baby sister for a few minutes then walked into his bedroom to test the waters. Which were no warmer in the bedroom than they were in the hallway. The argument was vicious and only ended when Lucia left for the couch and yelled at him to stay away.

After that, to keep Lucia off his back, he came home earlier. Instead of drinking at a bar, he drank a few beers in his truck as he drove home. *I can't believe I'm not even allowed to sit down for a beer with friends after work.* The slow burn of resentment remained in his gut.

A few drinks after lunch became a habit. Stopping at the bar made him late for service calls, and he was reprimanded. He tried to return to not drinking until work was finished and found he couldn't. The only thing to do was to keep a supply of beer ready to gulp down after lunch. He concealed a six-pack in his company jacket and carried the jacket into the service truck each morning.

A year went by on that routine. Then, one afternoon dispatch called him. He needed to report to the office right away to meet with his supervisor, Dan.

“Sit down, Alex.”

Alex sat down. He’d figured the boom was about to be lowered but Dan didn’t seem to be too troubled.

“Well, I got off the phone with the lady where you made your last service call. She said she smelled alcohol on your breath and wasn’t very happy about it.”

There was no choice but to lie. Alex cringed inside, as he respected his boss.

“I haven’t been drinking today. I did have a few beers last night. Maybe I still smelled like alcohol earlier, I don’t know.”

“Hell Alex, you know I like to drink as much as anybody. And you’re a good worker. Even that lady had no complaints about your work. I’m not even going to write this up. But I will tell you. I’ve had an idea you might be drinking during the day. Friend to friend, don’t do it. Do your drinking after work. If I get another complaint, we’re going to have to do things differently.”

“I understand. There won’t be any more problems.”

Sweating and red-faced, Alex walked outside. The dark cloud hanging in the back of his mind seemed to have grown. Disaster was just up ahead. *I can’t keep doing this. I’m gonna lose my job and maybe my family.*

Summoning all his will, he stayed sober for almost three days. Lucia was delighted and let him know it. On day three, his skin crawled and his mouth watered for a drink. He pulled his service truck to a tree-lined curb just around the corner from his next job. He looked at the greenery outside then looked at himself in the rear-view mirror. He had a momentary urge to smash his head against the dash.

This doesn’t make sense at all. The wife and I are getting along great now. My job’s safe. I should be feeling great. I’m miserable. I’m going to go nuts if I don’t have a few drinks today.

Alex was consumed by one thought—should he drink or not? His mind tortured him. It was some kind of trap. He needed alcohol, yet the world was putting all these consequences on him.

Suddenly his mind relaxed. *I'm worrying about this way too much. I just need to stick to drinking after work.* He looked outside and got his bearings. Two more stops. He felt explosively happy as if the relief was already entering his body. Freedom would come in a little over an hour.

He hit the bar immediately after work, swearing to himself he would stay only a half hour. Just before entering, his made a plan. *Two beers and don't forget to hide the smell or you'll really catch it from Lucia, you idiot.*

Seven beers later, he headed home. This time he didn't catch anything from Lucia except a goodbye.

Even fortified with the alcohol, Alex felt a chill run through him as he watched her gather up the kids. He stood in the hallway, as if to block the front door.

"We're going to my mom's. Leave me alone." She headed towards the door with the baby in her arms. Makenzye followed along tearfully.

Alex reached down to scoop her up, but Lucia led her away and out the door.

Texts later to his wife went unanswered.

He made sure to be home before 6:00 p.m. the next day. His family was home, but Lucia refused to talk to him. The cracks in the marriage were showing, and both felt powerless to keep them from widening further.

For a few weeks, he fought to avoid drinking until after work. Then he went back to smuggling in some beers to the service truck for use after lunch.

Irritability was overtaking him. Nerves jangled when he awoke. The drink urge was hitting him by mid-morning. He couldn't stand the sight of anyone until he'd downed a few beers.

Alex came into the company office and avoided eye contact with the two receptionists he had known several years. A large wall calendar showed his to-do list.

But it felt like the wall was throbbing in and out towards him. His hand shook as he pulled out his small notepad and began writing.

He glanced over and saw they were both watching him. "What? Can I help you?"

One of the women chuckled. "Well, I guess someone didn't sleep well last night."

"Yeah, whatever." He walked out and got into his service truck.

Alex sat in the company parking lot. He head-butted the steering wheel. His nerves were shot.

"I hate this place!" The words came out in a roar. It didn't matter. Nothing did. It was lose/lose all over.

I can't go through life like this. I have a right to be happy.

With a sense of dread hovering nearby, he drove to a convenience store a few miles away and bought a six-pack of sixteen-ounce Coors Light. He guzzled two of them as he drove, careful to observe for police in all directions. Concealing the remaining cans under his jacket, he determined to drink only two more after lunch.

"We'll call that a two-fer. Two in the morning, two after lunch and two after work." He laughed out loud and headed to his first stop of the day.

Carrying beer in his truck and guzzling them while driving became dangerous. Beer was taking too long to produce the desired effect anyway. Alex changed tactics, drinking a couple large slugs of bourbon at home in the morning.

He kept his stash in a toolbox in the garage, along with some mouthwash. Alex was rather proud of his careful planning.

He noticed Lucia's coldness towards him most at night when he wanted to be with her. Over and over he made the same tired promises and excuses. The ties that bound them were frayed and near to disintegrating.

Every morning when he woke up, Alex was overcome by a sickly dread, overlaid with guilt and terror. Knowledge that he was ruining things was supplanted by the overwhelming need for a drink. He would stand up shakily and head for the garage where relief awaited.

The morning bourbon worked well for a while. The hard part was waiting for lunch and the next go-round. Week by week, the hard part grew harder. Around 11:00 a.m. Alex found he was tired and depressed, as though all energy had been stripped from him. In the late morning, he fought the urge to drink. More and more often, he lost the fight.

One late afternoon, he walked out of a bar to get back to work. His supervisor and the company boss stood outside his service truck! Alex walked over, emotions divided. Part of him didn't care about them or the job. Another part felt a fear the alcohol couldn't totally push down.

Dan looked sad, more than angry or shocked. "Hello, Alex. Having a few drinks before you get back to work?"

He didn't reply.

The company's owner stepped to the front. "Give me your keys to the service truck. You're going to ride back with Dan."

Alex looked over at his boss, feeling very low and ashamed.

"Dan, I, uh, I'm sorry. I really am. You've been an awesome boss, and I didn't mean to let you down."

"I'm sorry too, Alex. There's nothing I can do now."

"What made you all show up at that bar? Did someone complain again?"

"Nope. We had someone follow you this week. He thought he saw you drinking in your truck, but he wasn't sure. The owner would've tested your breath at the end of the day if we hadn't caught you stopping off like this."

Neither spoke the rest of the way. They walked into the office. A somber silence hung in the air. One of the receptionists was crying.

The only protest he made over the firing was to ask if he couldn't have a chance by going to treatment.

The owner was dismissive. “We’re done. This has been going on far too long. We’re going to have to let you go. You can call someone for a ride home or someone here will drive you. Get some help.”

Lucia didn’t answer his call, so Dan drove him home. On the way, they passed a couple of bars, then a convenience store where Alex had often purchased alcohol. He was sweating. He needed four or five quick drinks, and just now his bourbon stash was gone. He thought about asking Dan to stop, all the while knowing how ridiculous the idea was. Then a thought popped into his mind. *Bob just up the street might be home. I’ll walk over to his shop and have a few with him before I go home.*

“Dan, drop me off a block away from my house, would ya? I want to walk around for a minute, clear my head.”

REFLECT…

"A happier life is waiting for you, but it won’t just fall into your lap. You will have to put effort into building new ways and spending time with new people."

Do you know someone who is losing all the good things, including people, in their life? Someone hitting rock-bottom?

You can’t persuade anyone to become sober.

Losing good things in your life hurts. One by one, the people and things you care about the most are driven away.

You can get off the downward elevator if you really want to do by taking action. Staying on the elevator means more drop- offs, more painful losses. Please take a few minutes to let things sink in. Ask yourself if you are willing to do something different. Then continue reading.

APPLY…

- Recovery starts with honesty about your problem.

It takes courage to face the painful truth.

Be honest with yourself even though it hurts terribly.

Non-alcoholics do not plan their day around drinking. They can take it or leave it without obsessing. Alcoholics take it!

Be honest with yourself about things that are not working in your life. It hurts, but only for a moment. Without self-honesty, you won't be able to level with anyone else either. Feel your fear, take a breath, and make a start.

- To get a different result, one must do something different.

You do not have to continue the misery if you don't want to.

If you're hurting, please remember it doesn't have to be this way. You were not put on this planet to suffer your way through life. A happier life is waiting for you, but it won't just fall into your lap. You will have to put effort into building new ways and spending time with new people.

- Get evaluated by a substance abuse treatment provider.

This is a good first step and it will open doors to information and contacts.

A substance abuse counselor is trained to evaluate a person's situation to assess whether a problem exists and to determine the course of treatment needed. He or she can also help you understand the financial side of treatment, including funding sources that may be available. Getting evaluated is a good beginning.

- Consider attending Alcoholics Anonymous meetings.

You may find a new way of living that will not only keep you sober,

but make you happy about it.

Alcoholics Anonymous exists to help people who have a desire to stop drinking alcohol. It's not the "only way" to get sober, but for many members it is the only way that lasts.

Please do not go to one meeting and then decide whether it's for you or not. Go to several different meetings; some groups will feel more comfortable and relatable than others. Listen to the stories and try to identify if you can. Talk to someone who seemed sincere and solid in recovery after a meeting. Find a sponsor as soon as possible. A sponsor is simply a person who will help you work the twelve steps.

In other words, absorb A.A. for a period of time. With that perspective, you can take a look at your progress and decide whether to continue attending.

RESOURCE TOOLBOX

- Alcoholics Anonymous (AA), World Services, Inc., P.O. Box 459 Grand Central Station, New York, NY 10163. www.aa.org. AA also has an app called "Meeting Guide" to help people find the meeting rooms.
- Substance Abuse and Mental Health Services Administration, U.S. Department of Health and Human Services. (SAMHSA). (samhsa.gov).

PRESCRIPTION FOR ABUSE:

Drug Addiction Overtakes Mom

"For in this hope we were saved. But hope that is seen is no hope at all. Who hopes for what they already have?"

Romans 8:24 (NIV)

She watched her boys walk to the bus stop. Her youngest was in kindergarten. Devin turned around one last time.

"Bye, Mom."

"Bye, little man. Love you!"

Cody was eleven, and he did not look back at his mother.

Liz went back inside and waded through the mess that her living room had become lately. This was going to be a fabulous day. No pressures at all. *I'm gonna do fine; I don't need any pills today.*

The phone rang as she was watching TV. Another debt collector, the third one calling lately. Her body stiffened. Suddenly, she felt cold.

Most times, she hung up immediately. Something in the caller's tone kept her on the line. "Is this Liz Dent?"

"Yes."

"Ma'am, I am from Conglomerate Credit Services. This is an attempt to collect a debt. You have not made payment on this debt in over six months. With interest, the debt is now well over five thousand dollars. If our office reports this debt to your state licensing agency, your license will be suspended. Are you prepared to pay the balance today?"

Liz's neck tightened, and she felt a stress ball forming in her stomach. She held the phone away from her ear as if the problem would dissolve if the phone was out of sight. Finally, she mustered up the nerve to speak, although her voice was weak. "You can't do that. I have children at home. One of them has a medical problem. I have to drive him to the doctor."

"That is not our problem, ma'am. Are you prepared to pay this bill or do I send it to licensing?"

She clicked 'end call' and threw the phone on the couch. Her skin tingled, especially her arms. Liz went outside, looking around but seeing nothing. She walked slowly back inside and sat back down on the couch. Then popped right back to her feet with anxiety. Fear and guilt tore through her as she walked into her bedroom and reached behind some blankets on a shelf where her Oxycontin bottle was hidden. She looked at the container for a moment. *I'll stop doing it tomorrow*. Knowing it was a lie pained her.

She tried to stem the flow of thoughts. Impossible. Her brain just wouldn't shut down. *How long have I been crushing my prescription Oxys? Just a couple of months and I've had the prescription since right after Jarrod and I broke up. It's not like I'm smoking the stuff.* Two of the capsules were in her hand. Using a spoon, she crushed them to eliminate the time- release mechanism and swallowed them. Relief was on the way.

Ha, ha, it will all be better in a minute! It was. Liz shut off the TV and popped in a Chris Brown CD.

Twenty-five minutes later warm contentment swept through her, replacing worry. Liz tried on an outfit she had recently bought and called her friend, Amber.

As she talked, Liz danced around the living room, an elevated mood dance.

"You won't believe this skirt I got from Maurice's, with the boots. Come over. Maybe we'll go shopping," Amber said.

"You know I don't have a ride over there. Besides, little Cody's sick."

"I'll post my outfit on Facebook in a minute. See ya."

From somewhere came the sound of pounding. Circus performers were standing over her yelling. Some of them had hideous faces. Liz held her hands above her face to push them away. Someone was tugging on her arm and she roused dimly. Her eyes opened to see Cody staring at her. His mouth was moving but she could not hear anything. She sat up as a wave of blackness overcame her.

"Help me get onto the couch, Cody."

He pulled her up onto the living room couch.

"What's wrong with you, Mom? What should I do? Should I call 9-1-1?"

"No, hon. I'm just sick. I'll be okay."

She saw Devin standing behind his brother and extended her arms to draw him in. He climbed into her lap for a moment, then walked over to sit in front of the TV. Cody stood next to her, watching warily.

"Cody, don't tell your dad or grandparents about this, okay? I don't want them to worry. I was just a little sick, but I'm feeling better now."

"Okay, Mom." Cody's face wore a confused, fearful look.

Liz tried to remember what had happened after she took the two capsules. Her mind was blank. She went into the bedroom to look at the prescription bottle. One pill left.

I must have taken two more of them after the first two. What in the world was I doing?

The next day she tried to fight the need, but it was too strong. She crushed the last pill and swallowed it. She had to get more. She called her primary care doctor.

"My abdominal pain is through the roof. You don't understand. I can't function with this level of pain."

The nurse was sympathetic. "I'm sorry. There is nothing I can do. You have to be seen by your doctor to refill this prescription. I can get you in next Thursday."

"Okay, make the appointment."

Eight days! Life was hopeless. She thought about having a couple of drinks. *I better not. I might keep drinking and pass out again.*

She called Amber. Liz knew that Amber had a prescription for Oxy.

"I can't help you, Liz. But I know someone who can dial you in. He goes by P.J. Do you want his number?"

"Ya, go ahead. Thanks, Amber."

Liz called P.J. and agreed to meet him in the Safeway parking lot that afternoon. Then she called her mother, Jill, to borrow some money.

She started her car but didn't pull out right away. *I was never going to buy on the street.* She put her face in her hands as a coldness settled in.

The car was driving itself. There was no way to turn back, at least not today.

On Friday night, she dropped the boys off with their dad for the weekend. Hoping they would forget, Liz decided not to remind them to keep silent about what had happened to her.

On Saturday, the boys' father texted her; "We need to talk."

She felt the flush of cold anxiety return. The boys had told Dave. He called ten minutes later.

"Liz, I wanna know what you're up to. The boys tell me you sleep all the time. Cody said you were passed out when they got home from school Tuesday. You better tell me what's going on."

"Nothing's going on. I was sick Tuesday and hadn't slept the night before. That's all."

"Don't tell me it's nothing. You're loaded all the time on those pain pills. That's what I think. I wonder how a judge will view that."

Liz cursed at him and ended the call. She was loaded, but not enough to block out her fear. She was going to lose her boys! The jumping off moment had come. She sobbed uncontrollably on the couch.

It was all so unfair. She needed her medicine now more than ever and wasn't being allowed to have it. This was it, then. She crushed up two of her Oxys and quickly swallowed them. Then she began dumping the powder from the rest of the capsules into the toilet. Finality with a flush.

I will have a couple glasses of wine tomorrow to get through. It won't be so bad this time.

The next morning came, and she knew immediately she could not possibly get by without her pills. She fought the rising panic, managed to get the kids off to school, then back to sleep.

Liz woke up wearily at 1:15 p.m. Every cell in her body felt lifeless.

The afternoon dragged on as she remained on the couch. She heard the kids bounding up the stairs and tried to rouse herself to greet them.

Somehow, she drove the kids to soccer practice, then to the drive-through at McDonald's. That night she lay half awake, sick and anxious. Twice she vomited. It was no use. She was hopelessly sick and depressed. Anything was better than this.

There was no hesitation, no fight. The moment the kids were out the door for school, she left to meet P.J. and pick up a new stash.

Two weeks later she opened her front door. A well-dressed man pressed a stack of papers into her hand. She knew what they were: her ex was asking the court to modify their parenting arrangement and place the boys with him. As she tried to read through the papers, she felt a paralyzing panic attack coming on. She dizzily stood up, putting the papers under some of her kids' returned homework on the kitchen table.

Money to buy more Oxys, was getting harder to come by. She'd had to beg P.J. to front her the last stash. He refused to give her any more pills and threatened vaguely that she would "be sorry" if he didn't get paid up.

She knew her mother would not give her more money. Desperate and sick, she called her to 'have coffee'. An hour later she was sitting at Jill's dining room table. She tried to disarm her mother's suspicious questions.

"I'm doing fine, Mom. Dave and I are going to talk and settle the custody fight."

The moment Jill got up to go to the bathroom, Liz sprang into action. She rifled through her mother's purse and ripped out three checks from the end of the checkbook.

Liz tried to look busy when her mother returned. "I gotta run, Mom. Need to clean the house before the boys get home." She hugged Jill and left.

As she drove away, Liz looked back at her mother's well-kept yard. She hated herself completely.

Liz was inside a hideous dream. A man was chasing her and no one would help. Someone was holding her mouth shut. She tried to scream and thrashed about.

"Take it easy, honey. Just relax. You're going to be okay."

Dim consciousness started to return. She half-opened her eyes and quickly closed them again at the brightness. A nurse was standing over her.

"What . . . what's going on? Who are you?"

"You are at Meadow Grove Hospital, dear. You overdosed."

As blackness swam over her, she tried to lean forward.

"Relax and rest a bit, okay? You're not ready to be getting up."

Sometime later Liz woke up. She had no idea how long she had slept or even what day it was. She saw a gentle-faced woman talking with a nurse.

"What time? I mean what day is it?"

The nurse walked to her bedside. "It's Thursday afternoon. How do you feel?"

"Better."

"My name is Shirley Ambrosia. I am a social worker here at the hospital. Do you have any questions for me? We can talk whenever you are feeling up to it."

Liz tried to think. Her mind did not seem to be working properly. She sat up weakly.

"My kids. Where are they?"

"They are with their father. They're fine. I talked to the three of them a little while ago. They wanted to visit you, but you were sleeping."

"I'm afraid, uh, I guess I'm afraid I won't be able to have them anymore."

Ms. Ambrosia had a soothing tone. “Try not to worry, okay? Your kids will be back tonight to visit you. One step at a time, honey. Tomorrow, a drug and alcohol counselor will speak to you. Just be honest as you can with him.”

I am supposed to tell these people stuff they can use to take the kids away from me? It was all so conflicting.

Liz lay awake thinking. After a while, a feeling swept over her, a feeling of comforting trust. *I will talk to that social worker some more. She seemed like she cares.*

REFLECT…

Did you see yourself in the story? Could you relate to a part of it? I know. It’s so painful and awful to think about. It’s okay to cry and yell if that’s what you’re feeling. Do what you have to do. Be gentle with yourself.

There are people in every community living a happy life in recovery. They have friends and serenity. You won’t want to miss it! Are you ready to start working on building a new and happier way of life? Here are some tools you or your loved ones can use to begin. Please pick up a few and give them a try. Tools are useless unless they are used.

"Successful people in recovery learn to trust in something bigger than their own brain."

APPLY…

- Get evaluated by a substance abuse treatment provider.

Opiate addicts need a professional to assess their critical, first-step, needs.

Addicts often suffer from acute medical needs which must be addressed right away. Prior to even beginning recovery, many addicts require a week of detoxification in a medical facility. The physical and emotional sickness of withdrawal is a nightmare addicts will do anything to avoid. Typically, they avoid it by using more opiates.

- Face the fact that you need help and cannot solve the problem yourself.

Addiction is a monster, and it is stronger than you are.

Are you sick of being sick? If you are addicted to opiates a part of you already knows you don't have the power to stay away from them. Admit it—drugs have their hold on you, and you can't beat them.

Now you are ready to be honest. You are going to have to trust someone else enough to tell them you have a problem and need help. Accept a lifeline thrown to you. Pray, and pray again. Hold onto that lifeline.

- Do not trust your own thinking when it comes to drugs and alcohol!

Addiction is a problem of thinking and perception,
just as much as a physical craving.

Addiction is scary. An addict's brain wants those feelings of relief substances seem to offer. You may be rolling along, staying sober and feeling like everything is great. Then the desire to use suddenly pops into your brain again. You find yourself inventing the most absurd justifications to use, just like before. The obsession is stronger than the will. Please, do not try to fight it on your own.

Successful people in recovery learn to trust in something bigger than their own brain. They compile phone numbers of people they can call in moments of trouble. Above everything else, they place trust in other people exhibiting solid results during recovery. Many find spiritual help and refer to God or their "Higher Power" helping them find sanity, while removing the terrible obsession to use.

- Find a circle of people not involved with substances.

Healthy connections with sober people will change your life if you don't give up.

Millions of people have recovered from addiction and are living happy lives with the obsession to use lifted from their lives. They have found networks of people who stay sober and are supportive of their recovery.

Remember that anything worthwhile requires time and effort. It will not be easy, especially in the beginning. When you start to see progress, you will soon realize you are on the right path!

RESOURCE TOOLBOX

- A good internet starting point for information, resources and links to treatment providers is: www.addictioncenter.com.
- Mitchell, Tracey Helton, 2016 The Big Fix: Hope After Heroin (Seal Press).
- Narcotics Anonymous, (NA) World Services, P.O. Box 9999 Van Nuys, California USA 91409. (www.na.org).
- Al-anon (for those trying to help and survive a loved one's addiction). (al- anon.org).

A NOTE ABOUT OPIATES

"Opiates" are a class of powerful narcotic drugs that suppress the central nervous system. Opiates relieve pain and provide a user with a rush towards a happy, euphoric high. The primary opiate drugs are heroin, hydrocodone, oxycodone (including OxyContin), morphine, Vicodin, codeine and methadone. Note: The makers of OxyContin have eliminated the "time-release" mechanism, due to user abuse.

DRUG COURT:

Getting Ahold of Long-Term Recovery

"It is better not to eat meat or drink wine or to do anything else that will cause your brother or sister to fall." Romans 14:21 (NIV)

Paul Broncheau and Bennie Apodaca grew up together, as cousins and best friends. They played basketball together, used drugs together and crashed and burned their way into jail the same month. Paul entered drug court a few weeks before Bennie.

Even before he was accepted into the drug court program, Paul was feeling different about things. He didn't want to screw up the chance the court system was giving him. It was more than a fear of prison. A lot of Paul's friends and a few family members had been to the yard; it wasn't something to desire but it wasn't a huge deterrent either.

Paul and Bennie stood outside the courthouse, a stone and ivy-covered three-story building, waiting for drug court to begin. Another probationer called out to Paul, "You got a smoke?"

Paul handed the man a cigarette. Bennie was being his usual self, bouncing off the walls.

"Check it out. I beat their piss test. The water cure." Bennie leaned over laughing.

Instead of joining in the victory laugh, Paul shook his head. *That idiot needs to keep his big mouth shut.* A minute later, he walked into the building.

Later, Paul puzzled over the intensity of his dislike. He and Bennie had always been tight.

Paul had had a rough patch in Phase Two. His p.o. [probation officer] had accused him of lying about his whereabouts. Paul didn't lie, he really had been out looking for a job. He'd found one, too. Not surprisingly, the p.o. didn't apologize or give him credit. It made him bitter. *Bennie's right. It's a one-way street! When we screw up they take us down. When the system screws up, there's nothing done about it.* Somehow, Paul fought through the desire to blow the whole thing off, probation, drug court, everything.

One night, Paul was roused from sleep by the sound of pounding on the front door of the apartment he shared with his mother. He rushed to the door and glanced outside. Bennie was hopping back and forth on the porch. Paul popped the front door open a bit, and Bennie pushed his way inside.

"Check it out. Let's go up to your room." Bennie walked upstairs and into Paul's room. Paul walked quickly behind him.

"Wait a minute, man. What are you doing? It's frickin' midnight. You're gonna get violated, and I ain't messing around with that."

He saw the glinty, triumphant look in Bennie's eyes. *He's carrying!* Paul's insides felt frozen as though his energy had been siphoned out of his body. The room seemed black with darkness or perhaps it was shadows spreading across his spirit. He saw Bennie loading little rocks into a glass pipe. Bennie waved the pipe in Paul's face like a wand.

"Just two hits, man."

The pipe that pushed away pressure. Sweet, warm temptation rippled through Paul and time stopped. For how long he had no idea. Then he heard his voice taking charge.

"Get out or I'm callin' the cops. Now!"

Bennie raised a fist but didn't swing. He locked fighting eyes on Paul for a moment.

"What's going on here?" Paul's mother stood before them in the hallway. Bennie retreated down the stairs, cursing as he left.

A half hour passed before Paul's heart slowed to its regular rhythm. He lay in bed under a blanket of cold fear. He knew he had almost thrown *everything away in an instant. It was all so confusing. He had thought things were going well. Why was I so tempted? I guess it's true what they say in the meetings about addicts being powerless over drugs.*

The next day, Paul walked into his p.o.'s office. His hands were shaking. He told the man about Bennie's visit the night before.

"Well, in the first place, from now on you are not to associate with Mr. Apodaca. Period."

"He's my cousin. How am I supposed to ignore him if I see him somewhere?"

"Let me put it to you this way. Avoid him whenever possible, speak to him as little as possible at court and treatment. And if I learn of you being alone with him anywhere, I will violate your probation. Is that clear enough?"

Paul nodded. It was clear enough. *Maybe it's a good thing, too.* The thought surprised him.

Paul got busy. Court, treatment, probation, A.A. and N.A. meetings. Then a part-time job. Paul felt like he was trapped inside a maze of machinery; there was always one more gear to turn, another pathway to cross. He was often overwhelmed, but he kept moving.

Less than three months from his graduation date, Paul sat in a metal chair with ripped upholstery in the basement of a massive Catholic church. The smell of black coffee wafted through the room; an old-timer was readying things for another evening AA meeting.

As if the coffee had somehow floated inside him, Paul's mind went into full swing. He'd been surprised lately. Proud of his job. Keeping some spending money in his pocket. Physically, he was feeling better than he had in years. He'd even started playing basketball again. A thought struck him to the core. *Other than a brief moment when Bennie came over, I haven't been thinking about getting loaded at all lately!* The revelation amazed him. Things were really changing. He felt a churning electricity as if a motor had just fired up in his gut. He couldn't wait for the meeting to start. He was going to be one of the first people to talk this time.

* * *

Paul took a seat in the mostly empty courtroom to watch his cousin face the music. Bennie was seated beside his public defender at a courtroom table facing the drug court team. Paul noticed the judge's face wore a severe mask. The prosecutor and Bennie's probation officer waited for the judge to begin.

As distant as Paul had become from Bennie, he couldn't help feeling sorry for him. Bennie's face was flushed. Sweat trickled from his forehead. He brushed the sweat away and looked at the judge.

"What? I'm sorry. What are you asking?"

"Mr. Apodaca, you made it through two phases of the drug court program. In six or seven months you would have graduated. Then, you tested positive for methamphetamine. You failed to show up for scheduled probation meetings. What we would like to hear from you is what led to your relapse and whether you believe the program has made any positive changes in your life."

Bennie struggled to speak. "Well I, uh, I was feeling the pressure of so much going on. Meetings, probation, court, job search, no money. I don't know. Yeah, drug court has changed me. I know myself even if you all don't see it. I believe I should get another chance."

The judge and probation officer exchanged a quick glance. Bennie saw it, and his face grew taut with anger. The prosecutor continued to sit back in her chair stiffly.

The judge continued, as if reading from a script. "Well, Mr. Apodaca, the drug court team has considered your violations. With just a relapse, but not absconding from probation, we would probably have reinstated you. You were on the run with a warrant for about two months. Unfortunately, we have no choice but to terminate you from the program. You will be remanded to jail to await sentencing on your original charge." The judge stood up and the others followed.

Bennie scowled at the three of them. He fought the urge to curse at all of them. He rose and kicked his chair, prompting a jailer to rush over and grab his arm. As he was escorted out of the courtroom, Bennie said, to no one in particular, "They never even gave me a chance."

Walking out of the courtroom, Paul felt his insides grow cold and tight. *I could easily be heading to prison on the same bus as Bennie.*

A few months after Bennie was sent off to prison, Paul Broncheau sat in the same courtroom facing the drug court team. It was the first time Paul could ever remember looking forward to going to court. His sisters sat a few rows behind to support him.

The judge handed him his certificate of graduation. Then he stood up and hugged Paul. "Everyone here is really proud of your hard work and progress, Mr. Broncheau. Your felony charge is hereby dismissed."

Even the probation officer was smiling. Paul knew his sisters were crying behind him. He heard the prosecutor asking him to consider attending the next meeting as a mentor to some of the newer defendants entering drug court. He made a vague promise to think about it. He walked out of the courtroom, paused a moment and then went back inside. He walked up to the prosecutor and made eye contact.

"I thought about it. You can put me down as a mentor. I'll show up here next week."

REFLECT…

Do you see yourself or a loved one drowning in addiction? It hurts. The world becomes a tornado, painful and hopeless. Maybe you fantasize about a Malibu cure, safe and warm on the ocean.

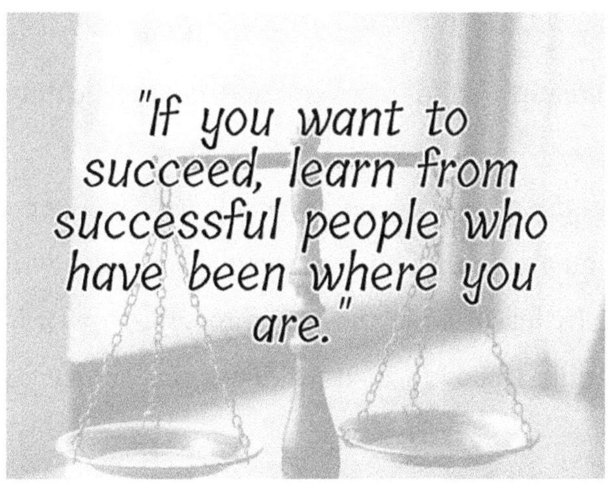

I know it feels hopeless. It isn't hopeless! How bad do you want to change? Take a little time and think about that. Are you ready to try something different? If you are willing to put in some time and effort, you are ready. Kind people will help you if you are willing to work hard on your own recovery.

APPLY...

- Do some self-appraisal. Ask yourself if you are in the program because the court forced you to do it or because you really want help.

Are you just working the system, waiting for the day you finish and can use again?

No one wants to go to prison or jail. From the outside, you may appear to be doing well. If it's only on the outside, it will not last. It will take inner courage and self-honesty to make real changes. You can only fake progress in treatment for so long. The scary thing is that without real honest growth on the inside, the secret, consuming desire to get high will win out again.

- Stop fighting the court system, even if you are only doing it in your head.

As long as you remain stuck in blaming others for your problems,
those problems will stick around.

Sure, it's the system telling you what to do again. Perhaps you hate the police, the courts, the whole world. You think it's their fault you're in trouble. So, no trusting them, right? There is another way. Some of those programs offered by the people you hate will help you if you give them half a chance. If you do not change your attitude a little bit, the resentment you hold will poison you. It will keep you in the same place that led you to your current trouble.

There will always be a criminal justice system. It will not always be fair. You cannot destroy it or beat it. The goal is to improve yourself so that you can get out of the system and not have to return to it.

- Spend time around people creating solid recovery and do the healthy things they do.

If you want to succeed, learn from successful people who have been where you are.

Find people who have been where you are and found a way out. Your heart will tell you when you are hearing the truth. Listen to what they have to say. Now it is time to say to yourself, "What he/she did, I can do also." Follow the advice of healthy people in recovery.

RESOURCE TOOLBOX

- Williams, Rebecca E. and Kraft, Julie S, (2018), The Gift of Recovery: 52 Mindful Ways to Live Joyfully Beyond Addiction, New Harbinger Publications, Inc.
- Alcoholics Anonymous (AA), World Services, Inc., P.O. Box 459 Grand Central Station, New York, NY 10163. (www.aa.org).
- Narcotics Anonymous, (NA) World Services, P.O. Box 9999 Van Nuys, California USA 91409. (www.na.org).

THE INNER WORKINGS OF A RELAPSE

I want to get high.
The horrors of the last binge
Fade from memory.
Fear takes over:
"Oh no! Here I go again."
My brain starts the endless debate
That can have only one end.
The want becomes a roaring obsession.
Justifications are invented and then refined.
Mental exhaustion and hopelessness ruin my spirit.
I've got to quiet the noise in my head.
One of my thin excuses to get loaded.
Will just have to do.
I make my plan
And use drugs again.

THE FIRST HIGH:

Where Addiction Starts

"Start children off on the way they should go, and even when they are old they will not turn from it." Proverbs 22:6 (NIV)

Sage jingled the coins in his pocket. He liked the feel of them. They meant a trip to the store after school. The night before he took them from his dad's coin jar. Mostly quarters. He was careful not to take too much so his dad wouldn't notice.

As he slipped on his backpack and opened the front door, he yelled "Bye, Mom," but he didn't wait for her reply. A few seconds later he was pedaling furiously towards school.

At fourth grade recess, he found Mack near the soccer field.

"Wanna ride to the store after school? I got some money."

Mack knew he'd be riding home anyway. "Okay."

At three o'clock, the bell rang. Sage and Mack hurried to their bikes. Sage led the way as they maneuvered around the flow of kids heading toward the street and the school bus. He steered across a busy intersection fearlessly.

The boys paused outside the store.

"I don't have any money." Mack said.

"It's okay. I'll buy you something." Sage walked up to the drink cases. The big 'M' jumped out at him. He grabbed a Monster energy drink, mentioning that "The 'Ultra Red' is the best!"

Mack's eyes widened as he looked at the cool-looking can. "I wish I could get one."

"I think they cost two dollars. I don't have enough to get two, but I'll share it with you."

They walked into the purchase line. Sage dumped a bunch of quarters on the counter.

The checker smiled at them as she sorted out the coins and handed some back.

The boys walked outside where Sage opened the Monster. He took a long drink, then another.

"Here, gimme some." Mack said.

Sage quickly gulped some more, then handed the can to Mack. As they finished the energy drink, their eyes dilated slightly. "Mmmm." Sage started to stomp the can down.

"Don't, I wanna keep it."

Sage handed the can to Mack, and they pedaled towards their neighborhood. "See ya," said Mack as he turned away to ride down his home street.

Sage rode swiftly up his driveway, narrowly missing his mother's side-view mirror. He jumped off the bike and ran inside the house yelling, "Mom, hey Mom!"

"How was your day at school?"

Sage spoke fast between heavy breaths. "Good. Hey, Mom, I need a couple of dollars for tomorrow. Me and Mack wanna get something at the store after school."

Susie grabbed her purse and handed him two dollars. She put her hand on his shoulder as he started to walk away.

"Hold on. I want to talk to you a minute. I don't mind letting you get something once in a while, but it's not going to happen all the time, okay? And don't be buying soda."

"Okay, Mom." He pocketed the money and thought about which energy drink he would pick tomorrow.

After school the next day, Sage and Mack rode to the store. This time, Mack had money too. Sage picked a Monster Energy Zero Ultra. It kind of looked like a can of beer. Mack bought an Ultra Red.

"What are ya guys doing?" A quiet kid from the school, Ben, was behind them in the checkout line. He was staring at their purchases.

Sage and Mack looked at each other and laughed.

Ben looked at them sadly. "You guys are lucky. My parents won't let me have those."

"Why not? They give you energy."

"Can I try it?"

Outside the store, Mack let Ben have a drink.

* * *

Sage was at Walmart with his mom. They passed by a display of Monster energy drink four-packs. Sage started to put one in his mom's cart.

"Buy this, Mom. You get four Monsters for only seven dollars."

"Put it back. You don't need that stuff."

"Why not? It's good, Mom."

"I'm not buying energy drinks. Besides, you have more than enough energy, mister."

A few moments later, Sage noticed his mom put a case of "Natural Light" beer in the cart.

"Why does Dad like beer, Mom?"

"Your father works hard. He likes to have a few beers after work."

"Does he get drunk?"

"No. He has to be at work at six a.m. Of course not."

"Why can't I have a sip of Dad's beer?"

"Because you're not old enough to drink alcohol. We've had this conversation before." Sage's attention shifted as they entered the cookie aisle. Then shifted a dozen more times before they finished shopping.

That night Sage walked into the living room to watch as his dad, Lenny, opened a Natural Light and sat on the couch to watch TV. He wanted to ask a question but was afraid.

"Hi, Dad."

"Hey little buddy, what are you up to?"

"Nothing."

Eyes wide open and electric, Sage watched his dad finish the first beer then walk into the kitchen. He got up to get a better look as his dad crushed the empty with one hand in the sink and grabbed another beer out of the fridge.

"Can I have a sip of your beer? You said when I was older I could." Lenny put a big hand on Sage.

"Well, how old are ya?"

"I'm ten, Dad."

"Well, you're old enough now I suppose."

His dad held the can toward him, and Sage grabbed it. He sniffed the top and looked hesitantly towards his father.

"Go ahead."

Sage took the tiniest sip into his mouth and swallowed it. He scrunched up his face at the bitterness. He saw his Father watching him and tried to remove the scrunchy look.

"First taste isn't so good, huh? Don't let me catch you sneaking a drink, you got that?"

"Yeah, Dad. I won't."

After school the next day, Sage rummaged through the kitchen to find a snack. His mom was doing dishes.

"I'm gonna drink beer when I'm older, Mom."

He scarcely heard her quick protests as he headed to his room to think about things he wanted.

Watching TV, Sage saw a football player doing a commercial for "G Fuel." A few days later, Sage came home with a container of powder called "G Fuel." He carefully spooned a scoop of his fuel into a water bottle and watched the green ooze downward into the bottle. He felt like a mad scientist in the midst of a secret experiment. After a minute he shook the mixture. Energy seemed to be surging through his veins, before he had even taken a drink.

He gulped some of his concoction and sealed the bottle. In his room, he was careful to put the powder under some shirts in a dresser drawer, and the mixed water bottle in his school backpack. He was proud of his work.

Another day after school. As the boys hurried through the store, they stopped in front of the "F'Real" milkshake dispenser. No new flavors today. They made their way to the beverage aisle, this time stopping in front of the beer coolers. A 24-ounce can caught Sage's eye. He smirked at Mack, looked down the aisle and picked up the can. It was cold.

His heart was pounding, but Sage kept up the bravado. He walked a few steps waving the can in front of him.

"Come on, Sage, we're gonna get in trouble."

Sage pretended to drink from the can, then set it down. They walked toward the "Monster" logo at the other end of the aisle.

REFLECT…

Do you have a nagging worry about your child and energy drinks? Do you wonder what chemicals are in energy drinks? Do you ever think that your children are learning to self-soothe from containers filled with chemical stimulation? I worry about this a lot.

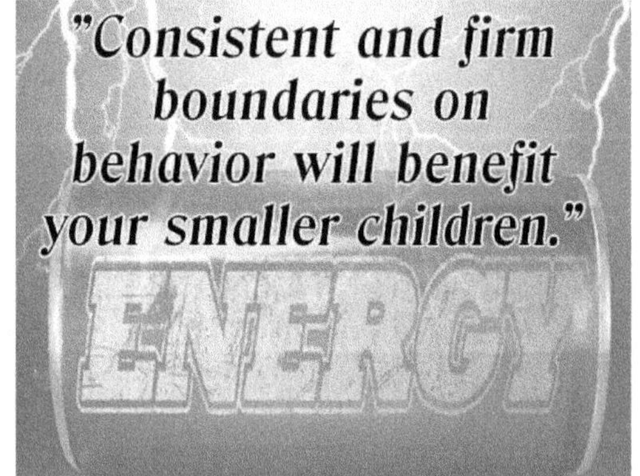

Do you feel like you've got to choose your battles carefully and this is one you can't win anyway? I have teenagers at home, and I know those feelings well.

Trying to control teenagers is like trying to swim up a waterfall sometimes. If your children are younger, you probably have a bit more influence over their lives. You are a loving parent with good ideas about what is healthy for your children. Please consider some small steps you can take to help your kids and somebody else's kids as well.

Look at some of the information below. Use the Five Percent Rule to do one small thing today, instead of trying to fix everything at once. Tomorrow you can do another small thing.

APPLY...

- Set strict rules with younger, pre-teen children.

Consistent and firm boundaries on behavior will benefit your smaller children.

It is going to be hard to do much about your junior high or high schooler's energy drink habits, but what about a fifth grader? Or a third grader? Kids are growing up mighty fast these days. Slow things down for them a bit where you can. The younger the child, the more control and influence you have at your disposal.

In addition to setting rules, do some reflective listening. What is your child saying these days about what is cool? What does she want? Listen for a bit without lecturing or correcting her. After a bit, tell her that, "I hear you saying ---, is that right?" Answers will tell you what is influencing your child. They offer clues to the future, too. Think about the moments and situations where child is most open to communicating with you, such as driving or playing a game.

- Use a less direct approach with teenagers.

The older they get, the less influence you have over your children.

So use your remaining influence carefully!

Waking up one day and prohibiting your teenager from drinking Red Bull is probably not going to be effective. Energy drinks will seem that much cooler to your young rebels. Besides, you may need to conserve your influence for even greater battles to be fought.

You might start by simply finding out how many energy drinks your child consumes each week. Is she drinking them every day? If so, you might focus your effort on getting her to reduce the number of energy drinks she consumes. Try to avoid getting drawn into a debate about the amazing benefits of energy drinks.

- Other parents have the same worries you do. Talk to them.

Form a united front with parents, teachers, and others who care about our children.

The culture is going to have to shift and that takes collective effort. Talk to others about your concerns. Share a story or an article about energy drinks and children.

Perhaps someone in your community would be willing to make posters or diagrams to show the effect of energy drinks on the human brain and body. Pictures are worth a thousand words. I remember how amazed my child was at seeing the image of a healthy lung next to a lifelong smoker's black lung. Six months of lectures could not impact him the way that one picture did!

RESOURCE TOOLBOX

- "Energy drinks pose potential health risks because of the stimulants they contain, and should never be consumed by children or adolescents." Dr. Anna Svatikova, et. al (American Academy of Pediatrics, May 30, 2011).
- U.S. Food and Drug Administration has reports of adverse health safety events regarding the use of energy drinks. (U.S. Department of Health and Human Services Food and Drug Administration Center for Food Safety and Applied Nutrition CFSAN Adverse Event Reporting System).
- Energy Drinks and Kids: What You Should Know, Henry Ford Health Systems: Henry Ford Live Well, Dr. Stacy Leatherwood Cannon, October 18, 2018. (Henryford.com).

"Energy drinks are effectively another form of drugs."
John Vincent, adviser to English government.

A CALL FOR NEW HOPE AND FAITH

If you are addicted to drugs, then getting high is the dominant idea today and tomorrow. This situation is the evil twin of the recovery mantra of "living one day at a time."

You really have two choices: continue to descend into darkness or accept spiritual help, which may come in many forms. Assuming your choice is number two, it is time to get outside of your own head and find something trustworthy out there. Look for people who found a way out and are willing to help you. Ask God for willingness to stay on the path of those who accepted help and found their way.

Please forgive yourself for a moment. You have not gone so far that there is no hope for you. Redemption and healing are available for you just where you are today.

INTRODUCTION TO PART IV: VIOLENCE

Small wonder that our society is a violent one. Our children view violence, more brutal and graphic than ever, as entertainment. In video games, they are participating in the violence, making conscious choices to kill human figures. And millions of kids are experiencing domestic violence situations in their homes.

The criminal justice system is taking steps to curb domestic violence, and some of those approaches are netting success. The broad nets cast out do sometimes snare porpoises with the tuna. Meanwhile, media/entertainment violence viewed by children is worse than ever.

A 2018 study at Dartmouth College concluded that playing violent video games "is associated with increased aggression over time."

Apocalyptic and graphically violent video games are extremely popular these days. The word "game" is misleading. These are not the board games of more settled times. Please do not buy into the mental trickery of thinking they are only killing "zombies." While playing the games, children do not remind themselves they are killing non-humans. The images and the "kill thrill" are imbedded into your children's consciousness.

The kill choices in games such as "Grand Theft Auto" are particularly concerning. Players have the option of committing evil acts, such as running over or shooting innocent people. Some of the video games available to children nowadays are despicable. Yet, children witnessing or experiencing domestic violence is of far greater concern. According to the Childhood Domestic Violence Association, five million children in the United States witness domestic violence each year.

The things a child witnesses from birth to the age of eight will stay with her the rest of her life. It is imprinted onto the heart. If a child witnesses things happening to attachment figures, the trauma strikes deep. Sadly, the outside world will only catch glimpses of the internal damage. When a traumatized child grows up and lashes out, the world sees only the ugly outbursts from an adult, not the damaged inner child.

Small children cannot make rational sense of trauma inflicted upon themselves or their loved ones. So it sticks, hurting and hurting again over the long years, creating patterns of relationship that create, well… hurts.

In almost a contradiction, the story titled "Domestically NON-violent" shows how the net cast by domestic violence laws sometimes snares non-violent people, as you will read shortly.

Convicting people of domestic violence where no violence occurs cheapens the meaning of the phrase "domestic violence." Our perception of the problem is trivialized, dulling our sensitivity when actual violence occurs.

Violence may be plaguing your family, whether on a screen or from real people. Perhaps you are conflicted about what is happening and what to do. What really matters is protecting children from violence and emotional trauma (until they are old enough to grasp the implications.)

Everyone seems to want to point the finger somewhere else. The blame game causes confusion and paralysis. No one knows what to do, so nothing is done. Start somewhere. Turn your children's minds to better things. Choose a step that fits your family's culture to reduce violence around children. Use the Five Percent Rule to make a beginning today.

VIDEO VIOLENCE:

Teens and Gaming Addictions

"Do not envy the violent or choose any of their ways."

Proverbs 3:30 (NIV)

Tyran sat in his room playing "Grand Theft Auto" on his PlayStation. He'd been sitting in the same spot so long his neck ached, but he didn't even notice. His eyes flickered as he maneuvered and fired weaponry. Red adrenaline fired through his nerves. A baby boomer would have described him as edgy and obsessed, but Tyran enjoyed the feeling.

He didn't hear his mother Patti's calls to come out, until she knocked and opened the door. He was annoyed.

"What?" He practically shouted at her.

"Your grandma's here, Tyran. Come spend some time with her. She's only going to be here two days."

"Okay, okay Mom. I'll come talk to her in a while." His eyes never left the game.

His grandmother, Delores, had always tried to help fill the void left by Tyran's father's disappearing act. Tyran adored her.

Patti and Delores sat at the dining room table having coffee.

"Is Tyran all right, Patti? He's always been a little withdrawn, but something's different this time. I know he's avoiding me, and when I peeked into his room to say 'hi', I noticed everything seemed, I don't know: creepy and dark. Almost devilish."

The words jolted Patti. She had the same thoughts, the same fear. She hadn't told anyone. Patti tried to keep her voice evenly calm.

"I know, Mom. I worry too, sometimes. But he's a typical teenager. He's never done anything really bad or gotten arrested. He'll be fine."

Delores was unconvinced. "I don't know what young people are into these days. Seems to me he's playing video games by himself all the time now. Have you thought about getting a counselor or church youth pastor to talk to him?"

"Yes, Mom. Tyran refused to go to counseling, and I don't think I can get him to go."

When Patti knocked on his door a couple hours later, Tyran yelled at her to leave him alone. He stayed in his room, with speakers blaring rap and hardcore metal the entire evening. Later, when Patti lay awake in her room restlessly worrying, she heard her son moving about the house. *He only comes out when he knows I've gone to bed.*

The next day, as Patti hugged her mother goodbye, the dam broke and she sobbed. Delores held her tightly for a moment.

"One way or another, Patti, you've got to get Tyran some help. I don't know, talk to the school. Bring someone to the house if you can't get him to go with you."

"I will, Mom. I promise."

After her mother drove away, Patti sat on the couch and tried to think. Her mind was numb and her body ice cold. She wrapped herself in a blanket and rocked forward and backward. After a few minutes, a strong motherly resolve came over her. She stood up quickly and tossed the blanket down. Time to do something, anything.

She walked into Tyran's room and examined things. The CD player on the shelf across from Tyran's bed was mercifully silent. Posters covered every wall. One of them in particular caught the eye: a full-sized photo of Tupac Shakur looking down on the room like a warrior-king surveying his realm. There were pictures of assault rifles, dark-clad ninjas, and zombie apocalypse scenes. The glint of shiny steel weapons reflected from all directions. Chains hung from the ceiling.

Tyran's PlayStation was in front of a 24-inch TV just across the mess on the floor that divided his bed from the rest of the room. Several first-person shooter games, including "Call of Duty," were on the floor next to the TV. The new baseball game "MLB: the Show" was on the floor, too. Tyran's grandmother had bought it a few months ago, for his birthday. The game was still in the original packaging, unopened.

Tyran's school notebooks lay on the headboard. Patti sat on Tyran's bed and started reading the scrawl on the notebooks. As she read, her eyes grew wide and horror mounted. Short writings, some only one word, were mixed with her son's inked drawings. One theme dominated both writing and art: violence. Armed ninjas poised to slaughter. Advancing zombies. Assault weapons of various calibers spread across the pages.

Most troubling of all was the writing. Tyran fantasized of being a destructor, a gladiator. Some scenarios were completely made up; others had him soldiering in war.

Patti walked in a slow daze from Tyran's room. "My son is messed up." She repeated the words twice more. Sure that she was about to throw up, she stepped into the bathroom and leaned against a wall. She looked at herself in the mirror and took a deep breath. *Do something, anything.*

Patti walked into her bedroom and sat in front of the computer. She googled "video games," "violent video games," and "Call of Duty." She felt more lost as she read. A lot of the Internet hits said the games were harmful to children. Others said more research was needed. There was even information that playing violent games simply released steam and so reduced violence. Patti shook her head and leaned back for a moment. *I am so tired of everything. This sure isn't doing any good. I need answers and help now.*

She looked up local psychologists. A few names popped up; she wrote down their phone numbers and started calling. It was frustrating. All she got was an answering service or a receptionist promising to relay her message to the doctor or therapist. After an hour, a psychologist named Peter Rangel called back. Knowing Tyran would refuse to go as he had before, she made an appointment for herself. *The expert will have some answers for me*. She grabbed hope like a lifeline.

A few days later, Patti sat in Dr. Rangel's office. Through tears, she poured out facts and fears to the therapist. She also showed him her son's drawing and scribbles. Dr. Rangel urged her to bring Tyran to counseling.

"I don't know if I can get him to go. He's fourteen. You know how teenagers are."

"Yes, I do. Please understand though, the situation you have described to me is extremely concerning. Your son's problems are not going to go away. And, yes, I am troubled about the amount of time he is spending playing violent games. For teens with social anxiety and angry frustration, the games tend to become obsessive and reinforce negative attitudes and behavior."

Patti grasped at a last hope. "He's never hurt anyone. Ever. He's never been cruel to animals. Isn't that something you would expect to see if he was dangerous like you seem to believe? I mean, isn't he just letting off steam playing those video games and drawing pictures like he does?"

"Not necessarily. I am not saying he is going to commit acts of violence anytime soon. I'm not saying he won't either. I am telling you my professional opinion is Tyran needs counseling, and I recommend you get him in to see me or another child psychologist as soon as possible."

"I'll try, I really will. Thank you for seeing me on short notice. I've been sick with worry."

She followed him out of his office and shook his hand. Before walking out the door, Patti stopped and looked at him through teary eyes. He stood there patiently, half smiled and shook her hand again.

Patti drove home. *That psychologist seemed to know what he was talking about and he seemed to really care. I'm not letting this go.*

Patti walked into her son's room and cleared a spot on the bed to sit down.

"What are you doing, Mom? Get out."

"No, Tyran, we are going to talk. There will be some changes around here. And if you refuse to talk to me, then I am going to take away your television, game systems and phone. It's your choice."

Tyran looked at his mom sullenly. Her tone and red-faced firmness startled him into silence. He started to protest and thought better of it.

"Tyran, I read some of your notebooks. Your writings are angry. And these games you've been playing. They are violent and totally inappropriate. I am so afraid that you are getting into things . . . I just don't know what could happen and what it could cause you to do."

Tyran's face flushed. She had been reading his notes! Something inside him made him pull back from the idea of screaming at his mother and pushing her out of his room. He felt bad inside, almost dirty. And caught. Even more surprising, he felt glad to be caught.

"I would never hurt anyone, Mom, I swear. I wrote some stuff, but I didn't mean it seriously."

Patti saw a glimmer of the son she loved so, so much. It felt as if he was returning from somewhere very bad. She hugged him firmly, and he hugged her back for the first time in quite a while. She looked at her boy through crying, foggy eyes. He was almost crying, too, her fourteen-year-old only child. Just now he looked so small, so helpless, so . . . nonviolent.

REFLECT…

Do you have a nagging worry that electronic devices, including television, cell phones and video games have brought violence into your child's world? Does it feel as though bad things have filtered into your home even though you yourself are not a violent person?

> "There is a fundamental difference between paying video games versus watching entertainment. The games have become extremely graphic, violent and realistic."

When I personally asked my young son why he likes to watch bad guy/shooting shows on TV, he said this to me:

"I want the bad pictures in my mind so I can think about that stuff when I'm bored in school."

Kids are telling us what is happening to them. Are we listening, closely?

Your worries are messages from your best nature, your heart. Take them seriously: they come from your love and concern for children. Now you can set an intention to move your family in a different direction.

APPLY...

- Arm yourself with information.

Watch the games your child is playing. Be snoopy!

Sure, it is "just a game" your child is playing. You are right to think it will not turn your child into a fiendish criminal by next Thursday. At the same time, maybe there is a feeling inside you that, quietly and slowly, something very harmful is happening to your son's brain. Your instinct is correct. Ten thousand violent images will have an effect on a young human being.

Remember, in a video game, your child is part of the action. In a violent video game, he is the decision maker, the shooter. There is a fundamental (brain-impacting) difference between *playing* video games versus *watching* entertainment. Many games are now extremely graphic, violent and realistic.

There is a rating system for video games called the Entertainment Software Ratings Board (ESBR). The video game makers have a lot of influence on the ESBR.

Do not accept the video game makers' misinformation. Decide for yourself what is right and wrong for your child.

- Do not badmouth video games around your children.

Badmouthing the games will strengthen your child's love for the games you dislike the most!

Do not lecture your child on the subject. Your child is ready with the standard reply. "All my friends play video games." Lectures simply enhance the value of the games in your child's mind. The games then seem ever more rebellious and glorious. Instead of confronting your child, be indirect yet consistent in applying the rules of your home.

- Redirect your child instead of banning all games.

Distraction is an excellent tool for parents. Use it often.

Get your child involved in activities that involve social interaction and movement. Put a limit on your child's time spent gaming and using/watching electronic devices.

- Try to eliminate or at least reduce playing time for the violent games, instead of battling video games in general.

Keep your efforts focused on the most concerning games.

Your child will probably respond to your efforts more positively if he or she understands that you are not trying to remove all gaming from your home.

If your child is participating in 130 "kills" per day, perhaps you might reduce the carnage down to ten or twenty right away. Use the "Five Percent Rule" to make a start. This means not tackling the entire problem at once. Momentum will build from your first step and further steps will become easier.

- Get involved.

It is rewarding and empowering to help others grappling with the same problem.

You are not the only parent who is concerned about this issue. Post on Facebook about the violence of the games and/or join relevant support groups. Engage other parents in conversation about their experiences. When you see a game that you believe to be totally inappropriate, alert others to the problem.

RESOURCE TOOLBOX

- Video-game-addiction.org has information and resources.
- Video: Sex, Murder and Video Games, National Institute on Media and the Family. (2003). Note: this is a disturbing and graphic look at the worst video games.
- Entertainment Software Rating Board (www.esrb.org) rates video games. Please be aware that this entity has been criticized for lenient evaluations of certain games and for a perceived conflict of interest due to ties to the video game industry.

ABUSER JOE:

Domestic Violence in the Presence of Children

"The Lord examines the righteous, but the wicked, those who love violence, he hates with a passion." Psalm 11:5 (NIV)

Ten-year-old Bryce had just finished lunch. As he started to go outside of the family's upstairs apartment, he heard his father raging in his parents' bedroom. A cold chill settled into him. He stood motionless in the living room, breathing lightly and listening.

His mom, Olivia, was talking fast, trying without success to soothe his father.

"Shut up!" came the loud male voice.

Bryce heard his parents' bed creak as something fell onto it. More noises. Then he realized something was tugging on his shirt from behind.

His three-year-old brother was standing behind him, arms raised toward Bryce, eyes wide open.

"Come on, Malakai." Bryce grabbed the little boy and carried him to the front door and outside.

"Where's Momma?"

"She's in her room."

Bryce put his brother down, and they walked down the stairs outside the apartment. Bryce kicked his feet across the dirt as he led them to the courtyard playground. Malakai stood next to Bryce for a couple minutes and then climbed onto the slide.

Another ten-year-old boy walked over to Bryce. “Hey Bryce, what’s up? Do ya wanna come over and play Xbox? I just got ‘Witcher’.”

“Not right now.” Bryce’s voice was barely audible.

Bryce kept glancing at the stairs leading to their apartment. He hated himself for leaving his mom.

I should go up there with a sword.

Then he saw his mother rushing down the stairs. He ran across the courtyard and met her there. All the while his eyes were on the upstairs balcony, watching for his father.

Her face was red. Already a bruise was starting to form. When Bryce saw her up close, time stopped. So did his breathing.

His mother’s numbed voice brought him back, though he could barely here her.

“Where’s your brother?”

“Playing on the slide.”

“Go get him. We have to go.”

Bryce hesitated.

“Go on! Do as I say!” It was almost a yell.

Bryce obeyed. He had to half-drag his protesting brother to his mother’s car.

As she drove them away, Bryce kept looking over at his mother, but he didn’t ask any questions. It wasn’t their first flight, and he knew they were headed to his grandmother’s house. Once, his eyes met his mother’s, and he saw that she was still crying. His eyes cast downward, seeing nothing, feeling the whir of the pavement passing by him, below.

* * *

As usual, his parents made up. Back home in their apartment four days later, Bryce tried to ignore his father by staying in his room. This was impossible. He heard a loud knock.

“Hey, buddy. After work tomorrow, you and I can go do something okay?”

“No thanks, Dad.” Bryce started walking away.

"Get back here." His dad's voice boomed. Bryce turned around and tried to keep his face blank, tried to hide the fear flooding through him.

"I don't know what your problem is. So your mom and I had an argument. Parents argue. Get over it."

Bryce mumbled and turned away again. This made his father even angrier. "Come here 'smart aleck'. You back-talk me again and I'll take a belt to you, understand? And don't start tearing up, tough boy." His dad's powerful hand reached over and tugged on Bryce's shoulder.

The boy fought to keep from crying or screaming at his father. He wasn't sure what emotion was trying to blast out, but the only safe course was to keep it in.

"Sorry, Dad."

"That's more like it, boy. Watch yourself. Now, tomorrow we will go do something fun. Maybe go throw a football around. Malakai too."

"Okay. Can I go over to Wesley's?"

"Yeah, go ahead."

They did not play football the next day. In fact, Joe didn't come home for several days. That suited Bryce just fine. Every day when he came home from school on his bike, he looked to see if his dad's pickup was in the parking lot and felt relief when it wasn't. The only one who seemed to miss his dad was Malakai. Sometimes at night the boy asked for him.

Mom put a plate of spaghetti down for Bryce, while Malakia nibbled on his garlic bread. Bryce blurted out a question. "Mom, are you and Dad going to get divorced?"

She sat down and looked at Bryce. A pause.

"I don't know. I don't know anything anymore. I don't even know where your dad is." She got up quickly and went into the kitchen.

"What's Daddy gonna do?" Malakai had caught the end of the conversation.

"Nothing. He's not going to do anything."

Malakai looked wide-eyed at his big brother.

* * *

Joe was home again, and a neighbor was over visiting. Bryce opened his bedroom door to listen. He heard his father boasting about a trip they were supposedly going to take this summer. Anger welled up inside him.

He's a liar. Bryce was grinding his teeth, though he wasn't aware. He closed the door to shut them all out.

A steady rain fell that night. The apartment was hot, although it was something else keeping Bryce awake. His parents had been drinking all evening. At first, it was all laughter and fun. They had even danced in the living room. His dad swung Malakai around like an airplane. Through it all, Bryce had stayed in his room until they yelled for him to come out.

Not long after his mom put the boys to bed, the sound of laughter turned to yelling. He could hear everything, his bedroom was right next to theirs. His chest was weighted with dread and his arms and hands tingled electrically.

His dad's voice was booming with the mean commanding tone Bryce hated more than anything. He heard his dad cursing and his mom pleading. Bryce got up and paced around the room as though he were caged inside of it.

What do I do? Hit him with a stick? Leave? Call Nine-One-One?

He put his hands over his face in anguish. He started to cry, then anger overpowered the tears.

"Shut up crying baby." Bryce slapped himself in the face twice.

Their mother's scream filled the home, then thumping noises. Malakai woke up. The little boy felt the awfulness in the air and began to sob hysterically. Bryce wasn't there to comfort him. Already, he was charging into his parents' room. He didn't know what he was doing. Later, he would have no memory of the events.

His mother lay cowering and whimpering on the bed, trying to cover her face with her hands. Joe was grabbing her wrists to force her to look at him.

"Look at me! You are going to talk to me!"

Bryce threw himself at his father. He landed three punches in the big back, then Joe threw him against the wall. Bryce fell to the ground in a heap.

Joe stood in front of the bed breathing heavily. A bit of saliva dripped onto his chin. Malakai walked into the room, wailing. Olivia used the opportunity to jump out of bed, grab the boy and rush down the hall. Joe followed her into the living room, cursed at her and left, slamming the front door hard as he went.

Like awakening from a dream, Bryce's mind returned to present when two police officers pounded on the door twelve minutes after his father left the house.

A smaller, friendly-faced officer spoke to his mother in the kitchen. Malakai was still in her arms, holding on tightly. Bryce sat on the living room couch. His lips quivered as he tried to answer the other officer's questions. His mind seemed kind of blank.

"First of all, are you okay? Your mother said you got knocked into a wall. Is your back hurting? Let me have a look at it."

"It's okay."

"Stand up, okay. I want to look at your back."

Bryce leaned forward, and the officer raised his shirt.

"I don't see any marks on you. Did you get hurt anywhere?"

"No."

"What happened here tonight, son?"

"I don't really know. I think my parents were fighting. My dad left."

"Did you see them fighting? What did you see?"

"I didn't see. I don't remember. I heard them."

"Did you see them in their room?"

"I don't think so. They were in there. I'm not sure where I was."

"Everything's going to be alright. I think your grandparents are coming over. You going to be okay?" The officer patted Bryce's arm.

"Yeah."

The two officers walked over to the front door and compared notes. Then the friendly-faced officer walked back to Olivia. Bryce had joined her in the kitchen. He saw that her left eye was puffy and swollen, and her upper lip had a little blood. Starting to cry, anger overpowered the tears. He wanted to destroy something.

"Ma'am, we are going to arrest your husband. Do you know where he might have gone tonight?"

"I don't want him to be arrested." Her eyes opened wide with deer-like fear.

"We have probable cause that he committed a domestic violence assault on both you and your son tonight. He must be taken into custody. Where do you think he went?"

"I don't know. He may be just driving around. He might've gone to his friend's house. Lander lives on the other side of Walmart. I think it's on Grove Street. Please don't arrest him."

"I'm sorry ma'am, it's a mandatory arrest. Do you want one of us to stay until your parents get here?"

"Um, no. We will be okay. I'm going to get the boys to sleep."

"Alright. We will patrol the apartment for the next few hours. If your husband contacts you or comes back here, you need to call us right away. That is for the best tonight. Will you promise to do that?"

"I guess so."

One of the officers pressed a teddy bear into Bryce's hands before they left. Bryce saw his mother lock the deadbolt, something she almost never did.

Bryce sat with his mom on the couch to wait for his grandparents. They had a two-hour drive. He got up several times to look out the window. Finally, his mom insisted he go back to bed. He joined his brother in sleep.

Bryce was dreaming an action dream. A man he had never seen before was chasing him through the apartment complex. He had no idea where his brother and mother were. He hid behind a dumpster. The sound of footsteps. Fear coursed through him. The noise grew louder. He awoke and jumped out of bed. Someone was knocking on the front door! His father? In a panic, Bryce ran into the living room. He stopped at the calm scene at the front door.

His grandparents were there.

REFLECT…

Are you safe at this moment? If not, please call 9-1-1. Take your children and get to a safe place.

Do you feel afraid, alone and beaten down? No one on earth has a right to make you feel like that.

Below you will find a number and website for the National Council for Domestic Violence. You can speak with someone confidentially. Most communities have trained domestic violence counselors or advocates.

You are going to find a way out of the pain and numbing hopelessness. Amazing, caring people are waiting in the wings to help you and the children. Please don't talk yourself out of taking a step. Make those calls today.

"You are going to find a way out of the pain and numbing hopelessness. Amazing, caring people are waiting in the wings to help you and the children."

APPLY…

- RESOURCES FOR IMMEDIATE HELP

Safety comes first. If you are a victim of domestic violence, there are confidential resources available to you. Call now!

National Domestic Violence Hotline: (800) 799-SAFE (7233). (800) 787-3224 (TTY). (www.thehotline.org). The Hotline is free and confidential.

National Coalition Against Domestic Violence: (www.ncadv.org). This site contains a lot of information and great resources to help you.

National Child Traumatic Stress Network: (www.nctsn.org). Scroll down the left to "Trauma" topics. Choose "Trauma Types." There is a section on domestic violence and children.

- If you are concerned someone else is being victimized, learn the do's and dont's.

Every victim's situation is unique. Find out what experts recommend as the best ways to help and support a victim of domestic violence.

National Coalition Against Domestic Violence: (www.ncadv.org). Click the "Learn More" bar next to the "Home" bar. Next, click "Friends and Family." There is a lot of information as well as SAFETY PLANS that can be downloaded.

Another guideline is available to help make decisions about helping a victim of domestic violence and reporting the violence: (www.wikiHow.com/Report-Domestic-Violence- Anonymously).

- Please: Protect your children.

Trauma witnessed by small children is an awful thing, and it will stay with them forever.

Don't hesitate. Protect your children from being abused and from witnessing abuse today. Lord only knows what Joe's father did to Joe. Who knows what Joe's great- great-grandfather, did to Joe's great-grandfather? What will Bryce and Malakai do to their children in nineteen years?

- Help for abusers.

There is help available. But what are you really looking for?

National Domestic Violence Hotline (www.thehotline.org). Click the "Get Help" button on top. Then, click "Help for Abusive Partners."

If you are an abuser, ask yourself if you sincerely want to change or just want to appear to have changed so that your partner will return to you. There are certified batterer re- education/intervention programs available in every state.

RESOURCE TOOLBOX

- National Domestic Violence Hotline: (800) 799-SAFE (7233). (800) 787-3224 (TTY). (www.thehotline.org). The Hotline is free and confidential. Click the "Get Help" button on top. Then, click "Help for Abusive Partners."
- National Coalition Against Domestic Violence: (www.ncadv.org). This site contains a lot of information and great resources to help you.
- National Child Traumatic Stress Network: (www.nctsn.org). Scroll down the left to "Trauma" topics. Choose "Trauma Types." There is a section on domestic violence and children.

FURTHER READING

- Bancroft, Lundy, *When Dad Hurts Mom: Helping Your Children Heal the Wounds of Witnessing Abuse*, (2004) (Putnam Adult 2004).
- Wilson, Beth with Hannah, Mo Therese, *He's Just No Good for You: A Guide to Getting Out of a Destructive Relationship*, Beth Wilson with Mo Therese Hannah, (2009), (GPP Life, Guilford, CT). Internet: (www.GlobePequot.com).

DOMESTICALLY NON-VIOLENT:

The Legal System Casts a Wide Net

"Do not pervert justice; do not show partiality to the poor or favoritism to the great, but judge your neighbor fairly."

Leviticus 19:15 (NIV)

LaRae Matheny's day started like any other. Had she known what was in store for her, she would have stayed in bed. All day. And all night.

There was nothing unusual about her day as a pharmaceutical sales rep. She worked all that Friday. A lot of miles logged, and all her accounts in order. LaRae was feeling pretty good about it. Time to hurry home for a few glasses of wine.

She sat at her computer in an alcove between the kitchen and dining room, returning a few emails. She placed a couple orders on Amazon. When she heard her husband open the front door, LaRae quickly clicked off the Amazon site.

The first couple of hours together flowed as smoothly as the white wine poured into their glasses. They sat on the deck as the night chill deepened.

The argument was, as usual, about money. Seventeen years of marriage gave someone a lot of inside information about where to poke and prod for the best reactions.

Steve wanted to argue. "You make good money. Then you spend it all. I just looked at the VISA statement. We owe over eight thousand dollars!"

"Don't blame me for all of this. How much of that debt was for Home Depot and for that money pit car of yours in the garage?"

"Hey, that car's worth more than we've put into it. Besides, we could have paid off both credit cards by now if you didn't have to have a new Accord."

His calm smugness upset her more than his words.

"I know. You have all the answers. You always do. It wouldn't have anything to do with your hours being cut at work. It's all my fault. Never mind. You're right again."

Anger flaming inside her, LaRae walked into the house. *No! He's going to hear it this time.* She stormed back outside and stood right in front of him.

"You know what, Steve? I'm sick of it. Sick of being blamed for everything. Sick of coming home from a hard job to hear how I'm not doing enough. As far as I'm concerned, my paycheck will be mine and yours will be yours from now on. I'm done."

Steve was angry too. "You can't accept it, can you? Can't put the brakes on your spending. I'm sick of looking at these ridiculous credit card bills for your shopping. You're just like your mom."

"You're an a… I'm leaving. I'm done." She hurried back inside, searching for her purse. It was on the kitchen table next to some of his classic car parts catalogs. She knocked the catalogs to floor, grabbed her purse and headed for the front door.

Steve followed her outside.

"Come on, baby. Come back inside."

LaRae ignored him. She opened her car door as he approached. He leaned in, blocking her from getting into the car.

"Get out of the way! I'm leaving." She tried to push past him.

Steve wouldn't budge. "You're not driving tonight! You've been drinking. Come back inside."

"I'm not drunk. Move! Leave me alone!"

She pushed him. Steve held onto the car door and braced against her pushes. LaRae gave up and walked back inside.

Across the street, a neighbor watched the scene unfold through half-opened drapes. He lived alone and spent most of his time complaining about the state of the world. The Mathenys' dispute rankled him. He called 9-1-1.

By the time two police officers knocked on the front door, things were calm inside. More than calm. Steve and LaRae had agreed to meet with a financial planner to work on money problems. They answered the door together.

"Good evening, sir. We had a report of a domestic disturbance here. Would you mind stepping outside for a moment?"

Steve stepped outside. The other officer, a stern-faced disciplinarian, leaned into the house and addressed LaRae.

"May I come in, ma'am? I just need to talk to you for a moment."

LaRae was startled by this turn in the evening. "Okay. Nothing's wrong, officer."

The officer walked inside. "Sit down, ma'am. Now what's going on here?"

"We had an argument. Really, that's all that happened."

"LaRae and Steve Matheny correct? You two are married?"

"Yes."

"Alright, you had an argument. Did it get physical for a moment? Did Steve strike or push you?"

"No, of course not."

"Did you strike or push him at any point?" LaRae started to become indignant.

"No! We just argued like couples do."

The officer's tone of voice became more challenging. "Well, how about you tell me the truth. What happened outside by your car?"

"Steve didn't want me to leave. He wouldn't let me close the car door. I don't know . . . He didn't hit me or anything like that."

"What did you do?"

LaRae felt weak. Her mind couldn't seem to focus.

"What did I do? I . . . tried to leave, pushed him out of the way and finally came back in the house. That's about it."

"I'm going to go talk to my partner for just a minute. Please stay seated here on the couch. The officer walked onto the porch. LaRae listened.

"What have you got?"

"I've got probable cause to arrest her for assault. She admitted to shoving him by the car. She is saying he never got physical with her."

"Yeah. The husband's statement is the same. She shoved him away from the car. He confirmed he never struck or grabbed at her."

The stern-faced officer walked back into the home and stood right next to LaRae.

"Put your hands behind your back, Mrs. Matheny. You are under arrest."

Her eyes widened in shock. For a few seconds she couldn't speak. As the officer handcuffed her, she managed to ask what she was being arrested for.

"Assault in the fourth-degree, domestic violence." He grabbed her left arm and escorted her outside to his patrol car. He opened the back door. Hand on her back, he nudged her inside. She scarcely heard Steve yelling to her that he would get her out of jail.

Thirty-six hours in a dingy cell. Her cellmate lay on a cot, scarcely moving. The woman somehow looked young and old at the same time. After a few minutes, the woman sat up and began screaming.

"Get me out of here! Come on! I need out!" Again and again, she yelled with accompanying moans like an animal in a trap.

The woman was oblivious to the yells of other female inmates to shut up.

LaRae was finally led to a video screen for a bond hearing. The judge released her on her own recognizance. Over a prosecutor's objection, he allowed her to return home and scheduled a court date for two weeks.

As the court date loomed, LaRae was nervous. She sat next to Steve as he called the prosecutor's office, telling the young deputy assigned to the case that it was all a "big mistake." She felt better hearing him say she "shouldn't have been arrested."

"Maybe they will drop it," she said hopefully, looking at her husband.

"All the prosecutor said was he would review the file before your court date."

On the day of court, LaRae took a seat in a crowded courtroom. A young-faced prosecutor spoke to everyone.

"Today is your arraignment. The court will have you read and sign a form advising you of your constitutional rights. Next, the court will ask you how you wish to proceed in your case. There are three options. You can request that a public defender be assigned to represent you. The Court will have you fill out a form about your income to see if you are eligible for a public defender. You can also hire your own attorney at any time. Finally, you can agree to schedule a meeting with me to discuss your case and see if we can work out a resolution."

Still hoping the case would go away, LaRae walked nervously to the table to the left of the prosecutor's table. Her voice quivered a bit as she answered the judge's questions. Yes, she could read and write English.

"How would you like to proceed ma'am?"

Eyes wide and still uncertain, she looked at the prosecutor. He didn't seem intimidating.

"I don't know, judge. I've never been in court before."

"Well, as the prosecutor told you, you can hire your own attorney, request a public defender, or meet with the prosecutor. What would you like to do?"

"Um, meet with the prosecutor, I guess."

"Alright, I will continue your case three weeks to afford you time to do that."

The prosecutor handed her a card with a meeting date and time. She walked out of the courthouse in a kind of fog, still unsure about what she should have done.

As she drove to the prosecutor's office a week later, LaRae steeled herself.

That prosecutor seemed friendly. *Maybe he will understand that I'm not a criminal. No matter what he says, I'm not going back to that jail.*

A receptionist took her to a large conference room. The same youthful prosecutor greeted her after a moment.

"Ms. Matheny, I have reviewed your criminal history, or lack of history I should say. Since you have no record, here is my offer. In exchange for your plea of guilty, I will recommend a fine only. The court will probably fine you two hundred and fifty dollars plus court costs. There would be no jail time and probation would be unsupervised."

LaRae's spirits rose with the "no jail time" pronouncement. "Okay, but would I have to plead guilty?"

"Of course not. You do not have to plead guilty. That is simply my offer to you. You have a right to go to trial, and we can schedule your case for a jury trial if that is your desire."

LaRae fell her insides grow cold. *Oh, no, I don't want to go to any trial.* "No, I just want to put this behind me. I guess I will take your offer if it means no jail and getting this done."

The young man pushed a form in front of her. "Read this. It is a guilty plea statement. You will need to initial here that you understand and are waiving your constitutional rights."

She placed a "L.M." next to the rights waiver. "And sign here."

She signed the form and handed it back to him.

The day before court she called the prosecutor's office. She was nervous about what the judge might do. The deputy wasn't available, so she fired a few questions at the secretary.

"Is it possible the judge will throw me in jail?"

"I can't tell you what the judge will do, except that she usually follows our plea agreements."

Despite all the nervousness and sleeplessness the night before, the court hearing went smoothly. She pled guilty and received a fine only. The nightmare was over.

* * *

A year later, LaRae sat drinking coffee and sorting through paperwork and the day's mail. Recently, she had decided to apply for a concealed weapons permit. She and Steve had several guns at home, and she had her own pistol in their bedroom. The permit would allow her to carry her pistol when she traveled for work.

Reading through the permit application, her eyes stopped on the words "disqualifying criminal offenses." Scrolling through a list of crimes, she saw that "domestic violence assault" was one of them.

Shock and dismay turned to anger as she read. She walked into the living room and tossed the letter into her husband's lap, as though it was his fault somehow.

"Look at this, Steve. You're not going to believe it."

He looked at the paperwork. Then he looked at her, puzzled.

"So, you are not allowed to have guns?"

"According to this, I'm not. No one said anything about it to me at court. You would think they would tell you something like that. My God! Have I been breaking the law all this time?"

"I don't know, but you better find out."

Alarmed, LaRae jumped into action. She found a lawyer online who advertised defending domestic violence. She called his office and scheduled an appointment. The lawyer listened to her story sympathetically. Then he lowered a legal boom on her.

"Yes, I've dealt with that prosecutor before. In my opinion, with this being your first offense, you should have been offered a continuance for dismissal. What that would have meant for you is that you would have had an opportunity to keep this charge off your record. You pled guilty. That means that assault domestic violence is now a part of your record. Unfortunately, that charge bars you from having firearms in your possession or control. In fact, if you were caught with a firearm, you would be charged with a felony."

Without hope, LaRae asked a final question:

"Isn't there something I can do about all this?"

"There is a procedure to set aside the conviction, but that is not available to you for three years from your completion of probation. Come see me then and I will handle that for you."

LaRae left the lawyer's office stunned and bitter. As she drove home, she thought about how to dispose of the firearms at home. "I will let my brother come get them until this mess is totally over."

Looking back on the "court B.S," (as she called it), LaRae couldn't help but feel anger at all of them, especially the prosecutor. "He misled me," she told her friends. "They don't care about fairness. All they care about is money and moving on to the next case."

REFLECT…

"Learn what you are up against before you appear in court or sign legal documents."

Maybe you are fuming at this very moment. Things are just not fair. You may be right. There's a lot that isn't fair happening right now.

Find a quiet place where you will not be interrupted. Put aside your anger for a moment. Think about the whole situation. When you feel up to it, consider how you can move forward and upward.

APPLY…

- Know your rights.

Learn what you are up against before you appear in court or sign legal documents.

Spend a few dollars in the beginning to save yourself from big headaches later. Lawyers usually do not charge much for the first appointment. If you have been served with legal papers or have a court appearance looming, seek advice right away. Before you plead guilty to a crime, find out all you can about the effect of a conviction.

A conviction for a domestic violence "DV" crime can carry with it the loss of the right to bear arms (Second Amendment to the U.S. Constitution). This is known as a "collateral consequence." All too often, the criminal courts do not inform defendants of other such consequences which attach to a conviction for domestic violence. Domestic violence convictions also carry a stigma tied to your name for the foreseeable future.

- Channel your frustration.

Frustration is energy. It can empower you or embitter you.

Your feelings are your feelings. It's your life. And your time is your time. Do not waste too much of it on hopelessness and negativity. If you use your frustration to gain knowledge and improve yourself, the bitterness will diminish.

- Use your experience to help others and to improve the court system.

You certainly do not want anyone else to go through what you went through.

Many states define "assault" as, in part, any offensive touching. This subjective definition, in the hands of some prosecutors, can result in convictions for violence where common sense would indicate no such conviction should follow. Help educate people about the court system's strengths and weaknesses. In so doing, you will be using your experience to the good. You will feel better for the effort!

RESOURCE TOOLBOX

- You will not find much reading material on this topic. A good criminal defense attorney will know the difference between traumatic domestic violence and an argument which resulted in an arrest. He or she will also know how to defend you.
- For help in finding a criminal defense lawyer: National Association of Criminal Defense Lawyers (N.A.C.D.L.). (nacdl.org).

A CALL FOR NEW HOPE AND FAITH

Life appears to be dark and hopeless because we bombard our senses with dark and hopeless images. Our spirits need filled by things of the spirit.

Avoid egotistical and mean people as much as you can. Step away from the electronic stream of mean and violent behavior, apocalyptic scenes, selfishness, and profanity. Our brains are being wired to thrive on disturbing vibrations, even as the central nervous system is harmed. That negative stream of images and thoughts feeding your brain is hurting you.

Then it is time to get fed with faith in loving God, in a manner that is comfortable for you. Put aside your intellectual cynicism and prejudice against organized religion and make a beginning. Your brain has been ruling the roost, and it is exhausting and disheartening. Let your heart take the lead for a change.

Darkness or light: what is your choice to be?

INTRODUCTION TO PART V: ANXIETY AND MENTAL HEALTH

Anxiety and mental illnesses are on the rise in our society. The loss of spiritual belief in a universe of order and love causes confusion and fear. The world seems unsafe and unkind. Meanwhile, powerful drugs offer the capacity to whisk a person from discomfort into a sense of bliss or invincibility. This is the backdrop for the mental health crisis occurring now.

We need a foundational purpose to withstand the shocks of modern life. Common sense would tell us that faith makes sense. After all, if you don't stand for something you will fall for anything.

The first story here addresses anxiety. Anxiety seems to be the young person plague of today. An estimated fifteen million Americans suffer from social anxiety disorder, according to the Anxiety and Depression Association of America (ADAA).

Anxiety can be a mild affliction that causes discomfort without fully preventing one from living and loving life. Or it could be a debilitating mental illness, such as Generalized Anxiety Disorder, Social Anxiety Disorder and other afflictions. Regardless of the phrase we give it, anxiety hurts, robbing us of sunshine in our lives. The world becomes an unfriendly place and harms our relationships.

Our second story in this section is about mental illness. Too often, mentally ill persons do not receive the help they need. State psychiatric hospitals have limited bed space. The jailers in any city will tell you that although they do their best, jails are ill-equipped to address the needs of mentally ill persons. Many jails are overcrowded. A lot of mentally ill persons spend time in jail waiting for bed dates, or for treatment personnel to evaluate them. This creates a tremendous incentive to shuffle people out of jail quickly, to accommodate new arrivals.

Medication can do wonders. However, so many mentally ill persons take their medication inconsistently, if at all. Many also use other substances that render their prescription medication useless, even harmful.

Anxiety/mental health problems and substance abuse often go hand in hand—a dual diagnosis. Academics debate whether substance abuse leads to mental illness or if an underlying mental health problem causes individuals to use drugs. Both theories are true. People who hurt reach for things to take away the pain. And the substances people use nowadays disturb and eventually destroy minds and bodies.

For many people, both issues need to be addressed. The further along these problems are in one's life, the harder it is to untangle and successfully treat. Early intervention should be a primary goal.

Fear is the bedrock where anxiety settles and gains nourishment. We strengthen fear by trying to numb out with our best friend, the computer (or increasingly, the cell phone.) "The computer is a new mirror, the first psychological machine."

If you are hurting right now, or watching someone you love hurt, help is available in many forms. Remember our formula? Here it is again:

Conflict causes

Consequences that require

Help which brings

Hope that leads to

Resolution.

The stories contain suggestions on how and where to get help. More than one approach can be undertaken at the same time. Find what works and run with it. Your heart will tell you when you are on the right track.

ANXIETY:

Young Adults and Overwhelming Stress

"Cast all your anxiety on him because he cares for you."

1 Peter 5:7 (NIV)

The more she tried to think about what to do, the more her mind disconnected. She went outside and cursed loudly. She looked at the phone in her hand and texted the situation to her best friend.

"Can you believe it? My dad's saying if I don't go to college this fall, they're gonna make me pay three hundred dollars a month rent and more for other bills. I'm only getting eight-fifty per hour at Wendy's. My paycheck is only about four hundred dollars every two weeks. They're forcing me to go."

When circumstances jolted Alyson into fear-mode, pressure flew through her like electrical surges. The circuit was completed by her iPhone, which was almost always in her hand. When troubled, Alyson's fingers sprang to life. She could fire off 120 texts in a half hour. All to the same person.

After a moment, Katie texted a reply.

"What are you gonna do?"

"I don't know. Go, I guess."

Alyson's fear mingled with hopelessness. Her stomach ached. She went back inside and sat, hunched forward, on the living room couch. Her left hand held her iPhone; her right petted the cat. She looked at the phone screen, which held no answers. A torrent of thoughts dominated her mind.

I'm not ready to go to college; I can't. Everyone's way ahead of me. I don't know what to do. I'm not smart enough. I just don't want to go this year. I'm trapped.

Fear swirled, and her mind raced. She was supposed to go to college, but she couldn't bear the thought of actually doing it. High school had been painful enough. Somehow, she had finished, remaining largely unseen and ignored in school.

The pattern was set. First came fear, then the sense of being overwhelmed. This was followed by the immediate need to escape. She got on Instagram and scrolled through pictures she had taken. She forwarded a few of them to friends. An hour passed. Only Katie had "liked" her pics. Wow, ignored again. The thought seared her brain. There was no getting away, nothing positive, no hope. She felt her hands tingle as the heavy mist of dread remained within her.

* * *

The day had started bad enough. She was due to appear in court for a speeding ticket at 9:30 a.m. She slept until noon. When she finally awoke, Alyson felt troubled. Something was wrong. She struggled to remember through the fog of thirteen hours of sleep. Then she sat up, panic stricken.

I missed court! She moaned loudly and her mother Lisa walked into her room.

"What's wrong Alyson?"

Alyson lay frozen with fear, eyes fully open like a deer in headlights. She didn't answer until her mom repeated the question.

"Oh my god, Mom. I missed court today! Do you think they'll let me come late? What do I do?"

"Court? What are you talking about?"

She had forgotten that her mother didn't know about the ticket. "I got a ticket for speeding. I was supposed to go to court this morning. Now I don't even know what'll happen." Alyson was talking fast.

Her father came into the room and looked at her sternly. Alyson knew something big was happening. As he started to speak, Alyson's mother cut him off, and took the initiative herself.

"I don't understand this at all. Your father and I are very concerned about you, Alyson. You sleep twelve hours a night and wake up tired. I know you always swear to us you do not use drugs, but we wonder sometimes if you are on sleeping pills. I want you to get in to see your doctor and tell her what's going on."

Alyson's dad lowered the boom.

"You might as well know. There are going to be some changes around here. You are nineteen years old. We are giving you a deadline of one month to show us you are either going to start college or start supporting yourself. If you aren't going to school, you will be paying three hundred dollars a month for rent to live here. You will also start paying your own expenses, including your car insurance."

"Oh, my god! Why are you guys laying all this on me? I have enough to worry about right now."

He rolled his eyes and walked away. "I've gotta get to work."

Her Mom remained standing there, watching Alyson. She had never seen her mother look or sound so severe. "Let's talk about right now. Right now, you are going to call the court and ask them what can be done about this ticket business."

They walked into the kitchen. With her mother helping her to frame the questions, she called the court. A clerk told her that Alyson defaulted, whatever that meant. She could put in a request to set aside the default or pay the ticket. Otherwise, her license would be suspended.

After the call, Alyson looked at her Mom. Each knew Alyson had no money for court. Her Mom's tone softened a bit.

"Alright, we'll pay for your ticket. But we are not back-tracking about you supporting yourself. You have one month to take some steps towards college or start paying your own way. Now I want you to make an appointment to see the doctor."

Alyson felt sick. She had to get away from her mother. Holding her phone like a security blanket, she walked into her bedroom, closed the door behind her and collapsed onto the bed.

I don't need a doctor. I just need everyone to stop pressuring me!

Her mother heard her sobbing and knocked on the door.

Alyson yelled, "Just leave me alone!"

After a few moments, she heard the front door open and close. Her mom had left. She got up and walked around her parents' house in a mindless figure-eight pattern. The future, the whole world felt like impossible terror. Alyson knew she was not okay, whatever that meant. She wanted a safe retreat, like a cocoon. *Why can't I be like Katie? She doesn't act like this. Maybe something really is wrong with me.*

She stood and did a quick turn about the room, as if she could spin away from the awful feelings coursing through her. Sitting back down, Alyson scrolled through Facebook photos and postings, not seeing anything on the screen. She needed hope, relief. She went outside and texted Kate.

* * *

A few days later, Alyson's mom scheduled an appointment at the local community college for her to meet with a placement coordinator. She had begged her mother to give her more time to "figure things out," but she'd gone ahead and made the phone call anyway.

Overwhelmed with fear, Alyson ate nothing the morning of the placement meeting. She avoided her mother's eyes as she left the house. No one on earth knew what an accomplishment it was for her to show up at the college.

She walked into the placement office in a sort of stupor. Later, she realized she had no memory of that part of the morning. Once seated in the office, Alyson sat motionless. She seemed asleep, except for her eyes. They were wide open, almost bug-eyed and fixed upon the college placement coordinator sitting across from her.

The man's formal manner did nothing to help her unease. She answered his questions in short replies, quietly, almost robotically. All the while her mind repeated the mantra: *Why can't this all just be over?*

Her fingers slipped to her phone, and she automatically started reviewing texts.

"Put the phone away during the interview please."

"With hope, faith, effort and time, you will start to find the happy life your heart is craving."

After what seemed to her like hours but was really forty-five minutes, the meeting ended. Alyson exited the building with a folder full of papers and joined a throng of college students surging through the campus. For a moment, she could not remember where her car was parked. She walked back and forth along the street until she got her bearings.

Climbing into the driver's seat, it felt like the air deflated from her onto the cushion. Alyson picked up her phone and started to text Katie. Tears started to flow. She pounded on the steering wheel, accidentally honking the horn. No one noticed. They never did.

What's the point of texting Katie or anyone else? What's the point of anything? Everything is hopeless.

She glanced at the folder the man had given her, and a thought flitted into her mind. Maybe she really could go to college. Why not, lots of people do. For a brief moment, she became aware of the warm, sunny day outside.

The feeling went away when Alyson opened the packet. Page after page of detailed requirements, paperwork needed, rules. She threw the folder onto the passenger seat, swallowed hard and returned to her shell.

REFLECT…

It's scary. Just getting up is difficult. It feels like the back half of your brain is completely dark, filled with dread. You feel paralyzed; your body and mind refuse to move. You are not alone. So very many people feel this way.

Do you sometimes have a small inner thought that there really is hope? Things can actually get better? That little thought is your truth, and more powerful than the anxiety. With hope, faith, effort, and time, you will start to find the happy life your heart is craving. Just think how nice it will be to reduce worry to a minimum. You will feel light with air surging into your spirit.

Are you ready? Take a breath and then take a step towards making things better. The second step will be easier than the first one.

APPLY…

- Get professional help.

There are amazing mental and behavioral health experts who can help you change your life.

Browse the Anxiety and Depression Association of America's website, www.adaa.org. The A.D.A.A.'s website offers helpful suggestions, links to support groups (including online support group) and other information.

Many mental health experts believe Cognitive Behavioral Therapy (CBT) is an effective tool to treat persons suffering from anxiety. CBT involves changing one's perspective. Consider giving this approach a try. At the same time, please do not ignore the other suggestions here that will help your heart to heal. Feelings come before thoughts.

- Get spiritual help.

Be open to the possibilities faith and spiritual growth can open up!

Millions of people have found peace and answers in their most desperate moments. Prayer, meditation, and spiritual study will change the trajectory of your whole life, if you are sincere and keep seeking God. There should be no conflict between treatment and spirituality. Good doctors were placed on this earth to help people in need.

- Spend time with people that are caring and motivated to do things you admire.

The old adage that your personality can be measured by the five people closest to you, has a lot of truth to it.

Take it slowly. For now, look for one person with a character trait you want in your life and learn a little bit from her. Along the way, if you have to stop associating with someone who is not healthy for you, try to avoid causing that person pain. Hurting someone else will make your own anxiety worsen.

- Do things that make you feel good about yourself.

Use time and repetition to your advantage.

Put your talents to use in helping others. Give animals your undivided attention and love. Spend time in nature.

Help yourself to feel better. Make an effort to exercise and get quality sleep. Do some of these things again and again. Over time, you will be surprised by the results!

- Find your own creative outlet to relieve anxiety.

The happiest people are the ones who are doing something they love to do.

Find out what your healthy passions are in life. Use the Five Percent Rule to start pursuing one of those passions. The Five Percent Rule means taking a small step towards something today. Small victories will lead to even bigger victories.

- Turn off your cell phone sometimes.

Although you go to it for relief and escape, there is growing research that the devices are increasing users' anxiety.

Examine how you feel before, during and after being on your social media. Try reducing your time on electronic devices, at least a little bit. Spend time with someone who makes you happy. Do this with the agreement that all electronic devices will be turned off while you are socializing.

- Do not panic about the fact you are still stressing.

Climbers reach a mountaintop only after many stages of preparation and ascending. Give it time.

The more you focus on being stressed, the more stress you manufacture. Besides, progress is not a straight line upward. There will be setbacks, and that's okay. Setbacks are disguised opportunities for more growth. They are also helpful reminders to keep using the healthy tools in your toolbox.

RESOURCE TOOLBOX

- The Anxiety and Depression Association of America (ADAA). www.adaa.org.
- A New Kind of Social Anxiety in the Classroom, Alexandra Ossola. (The Atlantic, January 14, 2015). Excellent article touches on the interplay between electronic devices and anxiety.
- A site called "Anxietycentre" has good information. www.anxietycentre.com.
- Panic Attacks Calming the Storm: A Journey of Hope in a World of Anxiety, Brian Ludwig, (WestBow Press, 2019).

FALLING THROUGH THE CRACKS:

Mental Health and Legal Issues Intertwined

"One small crack does not mean that you are broken, it means that you were put to the test and you didn't fall apart."

~ Linda Poindexter

He walked slowly towards a couple stopped at a traffic light in front of Walmart. The piled-on filthy clothes made the young man look much bigger than he was. He stared with an intense and imbalanced gaze at the middle-aged couple ten feet away.

He watched the passenger window roll up and heard an almost frantic "Drive!" The couple stared straight ahead until the light changed and they sped away.

Unruffled by the rejection, the young man walked back to his panhandling station. His sign had fallen. He leaned it against his backpack. "HOMELESS. NEED FOOD. ANY AMOUNT HELPS." The light was red again, so he shuffled toward the cars stopped in front of him.

After a few hours, he had a bunch of dollars and some change. He walked into a nearby grocery store and purchased two bottles of Thunderbird and a turkey sandwich.

* * *

Dustin Madera had not always been one of the nameless, homeless ones. He was strong and intelligent, with a supportive family. Dustin also suffered from bipolar disorder, a mental illness hard for people to accept and even harder to treat.

His year perplexed even the doctors. Whether it was the effect of a new medicine or a miraculous improvement, no one really knew. In his freshman year of high school, Dustin's mental health stabilized. He surprised his classmates by playing football and doing so at a high level. Students and teachers alike noticed how intelligent he was. Just as mysteriously as his rise to health, things started to deteriorate as summer rolled around. He ignored the coach's efforts to get him to lift weights and prepare for the next season. That was Dustin's last organized activity at school, and the start of a years-long decline.

By his sophomore year, there were minor brushes with the law. At fifteen, Dustin was kicked out of the regular high school and began attending alternative school. He not only resisted taking his medications, but began using alcohol, marijuana, and pills. It became an everyday thing. His mother, Marie, fought a losing battle to keep him sober.

"You don't know what you're doing to yourself. Mixing drugs and your medication is a very bad thing." She told him this a thousand times, but it made no difference.

Mid-way through his junior year, Dustin stopped attending alternative school and started disappearing. Marie's efforts turned to calling hospitals and homeless shelters. Usually, he would come home on his own or the police would call her to report her son was in custody. Dustin's crimes included assault and possession of methamphetamine. Marie despaired for his future. She battled depression and hopelessness of her own. Yet, she never gave up her advocacy.

Once he turned eighteen, Dustin's crimes put him in the adult jails. These facilities were meant to hold inmates rather than meet the needs of the mentally ill. Dustin shared cells with addicts and some very experienced criminals. Those times he was alert, he received an education of sorts in how to survive on the wrong side of the justice system.

Marie attended meetings with probation and court hearings. She always requested that he be given mental health treatment. Sometimes Dustin was referred to the local counseling agency, which had a contract with the county to provide treatment for those in crisis.

One on occasion, Marie was incensed after a visit with her son in jail. He had cried and begged her to bail him out, promising to do anything she asked. Marie barged into the counseling clinic without an appointment and demanded to see one of the counselors.

"My son needs to be placed in a care facility. That way he can be kept sober and the doctors can stabilize his medications."

The counselor was sympathetic. "I understand and agree with you, Ms. Madera. We have Dustin on a waiting list, but unfortunately, there are only two inpatient mental health care facilities for juveniles in the state. We're told that it's six months to a year out. Even that depends on continued state funding."

Marie began to educate herself. She spoke to experts and pseudo-experts. Many spoke of the "dual diagnosis" of mental illness and drug addiction. Each of them seemed to feed off the other, worsening it and making treatments largely ineffective.

She became something of an expert herself. She wrote letters to Congress. At Dustin's sentencing hearings, Marie stood at the podium and lamented the lack of services for people with mental illness. There were many kind nods directed towards her, but very little in the way of solutions.

* * *

Dustin was facing prison for burglarizing a residence.

"Deputy Prosecutor Couch will see you now, ma'am." A receptionist escorted Marie to a large conference room. A young woman wearing dark slacks and a ruffled shirt stood up to shake her hand.

"Hi, I'm Elaine Couch. I was told you wanted to speak with me."

"You're prosecuting my son, Dustin Madera, on his burglary case?"

"Yes, I am assigned to that matter. How can I help you?"

"I wanted to explain a few things to you about my son. He has very serious mental health issues. Here." She pushed a file across the table.

"He has been diagnosed as bipolar. He is on medications, but he probably hasn't been taking them. He's homeless. I understand he was found in somebody's house. He was probably looking for food and a place to sleep."

Marie watched Deputy Prosecutor Couch glance at the file in her hand then look up. She saw the lawyer's nervousness.

"I will be happy to review this information and discuss it with Malcolm Jones, his public defender. In his last case, he was found competent to stand trial. Mr. Jones has not requested a competency evaluation in this case. I hope you understand that the homeowner was quite traumatized finding a man in his kitchen. This could have ended a lot worse than it did."

"I've called Mr. Jones. He won't return my calls. My son needs drug and mental health treatment. He should be in a hospital. He has been in your jail for a month already. He's not doing well at all. There are no services available to him in jail. I have already complained about this to the county commissioners."

Marie noticed the prosecutor's eyes narrow. Then came the inevitable reply.

"I understand your concerns and I will address them with your son's lawyer. I also understand that the jail is not a very comfortable place. On the other hand, your son's extensive criminal history includes three prior felonies. He is looking at a lengthy prison term for this burglary."

Marie sighed. I knew I wouldn't get anywhere with the prosecutor's office. She rubbed her eyes wearily and kept trying.

"You're probably not much older than my son. I've dealt with Dustin's mental health issues long before you went to law school. I've tried to get him help. Everywhere I turn, I'm told there's no funding, no bed space available, nothing anyone can do. There's plenty of funding and bed space available to house him in jail. And prison too, apparently! How is that going to help him with his illnesses?"

The prosecutor stood up. Her tone made it clear the conversation was over.

"My job is to protect this community. I hope you can understand that. Thank you for coming in to talk to me."

* * *

In the control room of the county jail, a jailer watched a panel of sixteen video screens.

"Sarge, you-know-who is banging his head against the cell door."

The Sergeant didn't look up from his desk paperwork. "Put him in the isolation cell and remind him he is headed back into the restraint chair if he doesn't settle down. Then have one of the medics check him out. And get the on-call crisis worker over here to do another dangerousness assessment."

The jailer relayed the orders to another jailer, who was returning prisoners to their cells from court. Then he made the call. "The crisis worker will be here in the next twenty-four hours."

The Sergeant stood up and threw his arms up. "Twenty-four hours? Same old story. Around and around we go."

Twenty-hours later, the crisis worker arrived. Dustin lay on the floor in a padded cell. His energy was spent and he was sleeping.

The cell door clanged open as a jailer entered.

"Come on Dustin, you've got company. The county's crisis worker is here to help you."

Dustin sat up and looked at the jailer. He blinked his eyes repeatedly, as if to shake away their glazed emptiness.

"Come on. Let's go now."

Dustin followed the jailer into an interview room. A woman sat at the table with a notepad. She smiled and beckoned him in to sit.

"How are you doing today, Mr. Madera? I heard you were having a rough time earlier."

Dustin mumbled. It sounded like "Doin' okay."

She managed to draw him into conversation. He even promised to stop banging his head against the walls.

After forty minutes, she finished the interview and left to write a summary from a checklist of her impressions as to Dustin's dangerousness to himself and to others.

The next day the Sergeant read her summary.

The jail has reported that periodically Mr. Madera becomes frustrated and bangs his head against the walls. This has resulted in two occasions in which Mr. Madera suffered a concussion, though he did not apparently require hospitalization.

The jail puts him in a padded cell and tries to calm him down when this occurs. If he does not calm down, they put him in a restraint chair. Being restrained in this fashion upsets Mr. Madera even more; however, after a time he settles down.

Today, he was banging his head against a cell door. He was checked out by medical staff and determined to be uninjured. The jail requested a dangerousness evaluation.

Mr. Madera was able to answer my questions for the most part. His thinking was distorted, and he mentioned several times that he would be "sent home" the next day. Court records indicate that Mr. Madera's bond is set at $25,000.00 and his is trial a month away, so his belief about release is erroneous. I asked him where his home was and he replied, "the park." Jail staff informed me that he is homeless.

At this time, Mr. Madera is not a threat to himself or others. He should be monitored closely to make sure he is taking his medication and to protect him in the event he becomes frustrated.

The Sergeant finished reading the report and flung it onto his desk.

"Not dangerous to himself? He sees the medics at least once a week. This guy needs some kind of hospital. How are we supposed to take care of him? We are short- staffed and over capacity as it is."

One of the other two jailers in the control room didn't reply. He was hurrying out to the floor to deal with an inmate flooding one of the toilets.

REFLECT...

"The emotional pain of many people afflicted with mental illness is beyond sad. Faith can provide comfort and peace to hurting people.'

You want your loved one to get better. You try so hard, yet nothing seems to improve. Without your loved one buying into your efforts, he or she doesn't get healthier. Please try to put away blame and guilt. Give yourself some credit. You are persevering in difficult circumstances.

Perhaps you, as the advocate, are grappling with your own mental health. Please be open to trusting those who have your best interest in mind. Sometimes your own brain will trick you or lead you down bad paths.

I know there are no answers to the why questions. "Why me?" or "Why is this happening?" On the other hand, there is a growing understanding of the problems facing mentally ill persons and their loved ones. Advocates are fighting for more resources and tools. I hope you will tap into this new energy and get some help for yourself and your family.

APPLY...

- Take care of your own needs. You are in this for the long haul.

  Without self-care, we cannot help others.

- Look for the best professionals in your area and follow their advice.

  Finding an expert you feel confident about is critical.

A national organization called the National Alliance on Mental Illness ("NAMI") provides support groups and a wealth of information. (www.nami.org).

Peruse their site and try to connect with a group. Please be aware that criticism has been leveled at the organization due to ties to the pharmaceutical industry.

- Mentally ill persons need consistency and structure.

The lack of follow-through, especially in the taking of medications, is disastrous.

So many mentally ill persons fail to take necessary medications unless forced to do so. They believe they do not need to do so, and often lie about having taken them. This frustrates the efforts of loved ones and professionals at every turn.

- Do not ignore spiritual solutions.

The best doctors are open to spiritual approaches.

Miracles of regeneration and healing occur. The emotional pain of many people afflicted with mental illness is beyond sad. Faith can provide comfort and peace to hurting people.

- Continue to be an advocate for your loved one and others suffering from the same problems.

Society and the systems in place will not change without pressure.

The only remedy for people who fall through the cracks of society is unrelenting advocacy. In doing so, you will help many people.

- Make a record of what is happening in your loved one's life in court, in jail and in treatment. Create a portfolio of the mentally ill person's life, starting with a photograph of him or her. Exhibit A should be the psychologist/psychiatrist's evaluation and diagnoses. Document the failures of care. You will need this information to get people's attention.

RESOURCE TOOLBOX

- National Alliance on Mental Illness (NAMI). www.nami.org.
- National Institute of Mental Health (NIMH). nimh.nih.gov.

A CALL FOR NEW HOPE AND FAITH

Are you, dear reader, hurting for yourself or someone else right now? Perhaps there awaits the soothing voices and loving arms of people who care, people who have faith. It doesn't matter whether you first find faith and then find real (not virtual) human companionship. Or whether your real connections with people lead you to faith. Start somewhere via the Five Percent Rule, and watch things get better.

Beginning your faith journey is not as hard as it seems. Probably, you already demonstrate faith at some level.

For example, you meet a person for the first time, with the title of "doctor." Perhaps because of this, you have immediate faith in this person's ability to help you. That faith, or belief if you prefer, actually magnifies the doctor's treatment effectiveness. Without that faith, you might not even bother to fill the prescription for medicine prescribed to you. So, faith in something or someone is already a part of your life. You are not on earth by accident! God loves you and includes a good and loving purpose for you.

You will feel tremendous relief if you let God do some of the heavy lifting. Let God get to work on that bedrock in your soul called fear. Spirit offers a quiet grip on you, supporting you to quit paralyzing your decision making, or letting things churn inside your mind. A spiritual program of action can quiet that fearful corrosive force.

My prayer for those hurting right now is that they will find the help they need. May you find new hope so that you can feel the sunshine streaming down upon you.

ABOUT THE AUTHOR

Neil Presley Cox is a husband, father, author, and a very busy family law and companion criminal defense attorney, licensed in the states of Washington and Idaho.

His latest book, ***HOPE LINES: 18 Stories of Families in Trouble and the Help They Need in Spirit, Sense and Law***, addresses modern personal and family challenges, while providing practical answers to those problems, with a spiritual flavor.

Growing up in Fremont, California, he attended college at Cal State Hayward before transferring to the University of Idaho, earning a BA in History prior to pursuing a law degree.

After earning his J.D. (Juris Doctorate) law degree from the University of Idaho in 1994, he began his career with the Henderson and Grow law firm of Clarkston, Washington. After working there until 2000, he opened his own law office, also in Clarkston.

According to Neil, his specialty in family law evolved organically. He started as a 'jack of all trades', but one kind of referral kept coming (and coming!). Those he assisted in getting through the legal quagmire appreciated his positive, genuine assistance so much, they could not wait to tell others in trouble or crisis to "call the lawyer with a heart".

Neil's giving and compassionate parents were the role models underlying his patient and deeply empathetic approach to working with people in crisis.

To this day, his practice works to incorporate the spiritual teachings of Jesus, while helping those who struggle with addiction, abuse, divorce, custody issues, drugs, and any number of family crises. His goal is to lead them along the court system conveyor belt with a minimum of psychic damage, so they can still feel HOPE when the nightmare is over.

Professional accolades include several winning appeals published in the legal system lexicon, including one with the Washington Supreme Court.

Unfortunately, with a working life steeped constantly in client struggles, Neil fell prey to his own experience with alcohol addiction as a coping mechanism. His story of recovery (18 years sober as of 2022) is summarized in the Introduction to ***Hope Lines***, and becomes part of his real-life incentive to write this resource.

Neil's first book was ***Alcoholprism***, featuring poetry for people in all aspects of recovery. The poems emerged during his recovery meetings, where words and phrases would seep into his head—and in true artist-story form—he started writing them down.

- IndieReader gives ***Alcoholprism*** four stars, and a prestigious "IR Approved" designation. More info at https://indiereader.com/book_review/alcoholprism/
- Good Reads also provided a hearty review at https://www.goodreads.com/book/show/20670918-alcoholprism
- ***Alcoholprism***, the book, is available on Amazon at https://amzn.to/2ClaxmM. A 2nd edition is in the works.

In addition to his regular law practice, Neil serves occasionally as Judge Pro Tem for the town of Asotin, Washington.

A self-described fitness nut, Neil still enjoys playing basketball and regular outdoor activities with his family, especially hiking, camping, and backpacking. Time spent connecting to nature also provides a much-needed spiritual outlet, and recess from the steady flood of clients in crisis.

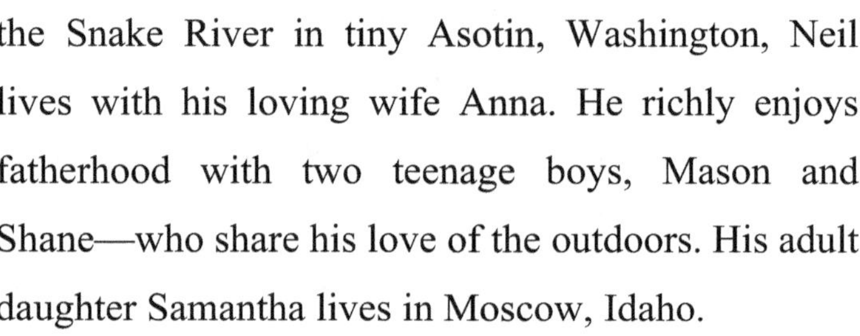

At his home along the banks of the Snake River in tiny Asotin, Washington, Neil lives with his loving wife Anna. He richly enjoys fatherhood with two teenage boys, Mason and Shane—who share his love of the outdoors. His adult daughter Samantha lives in Moscow, Idaho.

Neil and his family attend LifeCenter Church in Clarkston, where he helps with student ministries.

Available as a speaker to churches and other organizations in northern Idaho and eastern Washington, Neil can be reached at:

- Coxpresley8@gmail.com
- (509) 758-6092 (law office)

Besides the paperback and Kindle e-book versions of ***Hope Lines*** on Amazon, you may purchase the entire book or even the 18 story/chapters individually in PDF format on Neil's website. These make very nice virtual gifts for friends or family members in trouble:

https://www.neilpresleycox.com/hopelines.html

www.ingramcontent.com/pod-product-compliance
Lightning Source LLC
LaVergne TN
LVHW081259100826
845148LV00005B/925
9780975367605